The Virtual and the Real: Media in the Museum

The Virtual and the Real: Media in the Museum

Reprinted 2000

Library of Congress Cataloging-in-Publication Data

The virtual and the real : media in the museum / edited by Selma
    Thomas and Ann Mintz.
            p.   cm.
        Includes index.
        ISBN 0-931201-51-9
        Museums—Technological innovations.   2. Mass media and
technology.   3. Multimedia systems.   4. Information technology.
I. Thomas, Selma.   II. Mintz, Ann.   1947– .   III. American
Association of Museums.
AM7.V57   1998
069—dc21   98-5481
                                                                              CIP

The Virtual and the Real: Media in the Museum

Edited by
Selma Thomas and Ann Mintz

© 1998 American Association of Museums
1575 Eye St. N.W., Suite 400
Washington, DC 20005

Table of Contents

Acknowledgements
Selma Thomas and Ann Mintz

This book is the result of many collaborative efforts. First, it is the cumulative effort of the editors. We met in 1992, when we were both invited to consult with the National Museum of the American Indian on their future technology needs. We were immediately struck at the similarities in our professional backgrounds and agreed to collaborate on this book. We invited some of our most valued colleagues to join us in this effort, and we wish to acknowledge their contributions, not only to this publication but also to our own professional and intellectual development. We must also thank our editors, John Strand and Jane Lusaka, who took a collection of essays and shaped them into a coherent publication without sacrificing the individual voices and perspectives of the authors.

Finally, we want to give a special acknowledgment to our late colleague Steve Borysewicz. He was an exhibit developer at the Field Museum when we met him. He presented a paper at the 1996 AAM Annual Meeting in Minneapolis, on the museum's Web site. We were so impressed by his presentation that we approached him after the session and invited him to write a chapter for the book. A year later, at the meeting in Atlanta, he presented a paper in a session he proposed, "If It Works, Is It Obsolete?" It was another brilliant, witty, and provocative performance. He was killed in a motorcycle accident in August 1997, only months before his 40th birthday. His essay is a lasting reminder of his contribution to the museum field.

Introduction

Selma Thomas

"Media" is a high-concept term. We know media when we see it, but we are often confused when asked to identify its separate components. The television set in my living room is a provider of media—high-quality moving pictures with sync sound. The computer on my office desk is another provider, one that allows me to browse the Internet or to peruse a CD-ROM, with its high-quality picture and audio.

The presence of the Internet gives us more choices and our terminology reveals a new relationship between audience and electronic screen. The television viewer becomes a computer user. In the near future, the computer itself will become the television for most homes. The World Wide Web allows the user to become a producer. Create your own Web site and you, too, are a provider of information.

All of these technologies are based on some combination of image, text, and sound. All of these technologies provide information, whether it is the now-traditional narrative of a feature film, the multimedia choices of a CD-ROM, or the daily on-line bulletin board of a cultural institution. But each form of technology *mediates* information into a format that is accessible to the consumer.

Museums have adapted all of these media for use in exhibitions and other public programs. Inside the museum, installed in public spaces, they are juxtaposed with museum collections and help mediate the three-dimensional realities of the collections. Even on the World Wide Web, the referential presence of real objects and real experiences adds the subtext of cultural authority.

Selma Thomas is a historian and filmmaker with a dual interest in media and museums. She began her career producing documentaries for public television and in recent years has specialized in developing media and multimedia for museum exhibitions.

This book is a reflection on the nature of museology in the age of information. In the era of Disney, MTV, the Internet, and emerging forms of virtual reality, it is a fruitful exercise to ask: "Is there room for, a need for, an audience for cultural institutions that collect and interpret 'real' objects?" We ourselves, professionals working in museums, may have no doubt that the answer is "Definitely!" But to ask the question, even implicitly, is to provide a forum where we might explore the relationships among object, venue, and audience, and how those relationships are mediated.

We will examine the impact of "new media" on museums, exploring the many ways technology has mediated the real objects and real experiences provided by museums. While others have examined the changes that electronic media has imposed on internal issues, most notably in *The Wired Museum*, edited by Katherine Jones-Garmil (American Association of Museums, 1997), we will look at the way media affects the external relationship between museums and their audiences. This is the greatest and most underrated factor about new media: To produce and use media well, we have to define and redefine, question and evaluate our approaches to and goals for education and interpretation.

The authors of the following chapters are not all "media experts," and even when they have a unique expertise in technology, they do not identify themselves as media experts. Instead, their titles represent the many broad talents that any successful public program requires: managers, administrators, evaluators, education specialists, curators, and yes, one film producer. All these professionals bring significant skills and insights to the problem of developing and producing media programs for museums.

Ruth Perlin, head of education resources at the National Gallery of Art, Washington, D.C., reminds us that: "[N]ew technologies are not ends in themselves; they represent powerful means for attaining the goals of educating the public and integrating art into their lives." She speaks as an art historian, but John Falk and Lynn Dierking, principals of Institute for Learning Innovation (formerly Science Learning, inc.), Annapolis, Md., echo some of her concerns. Making the point that media is not the only mode of presentation available to a museum, they suggest: "The focal point of the experience should always be the object, phenomena, and/or ideas that are a part of the institution's mission." Addressing would-be producers, Ann Mintz, executive director of the Science Center at the Whitaker Center for Science and the Arts, Harrisburg, Pa., counsels: "The first question to ask is not 'What can I do with a computer' but 'What am I trying to accomplish?' The process must begin with the museum and its needs, and the first step is to define these needs."

But if we define exhibitions and other public programs as a conversation between an institution and its audience, then the museum's needs are only one concern. We must also address the needs of the visitor. Michael H. Robinson, director of the National Zoological Park, Washington, D.C., supports the primacy of learning by observation and experimentation over learning by survey and rote. The museum, he suggests, provides a unique opportunity, and venue, for observing and experimenting. Rob Semper, a physicist and the executive associate director at the Exploratorium, San Francisco, explores the role of venue in creating the museum experience. He writes, "Museum exhibit space is not a living room, classroom, theater, or office, and the media design rules, interface design, and A/V equipment that work for those environments will not necessarily work for museums." Judy Gradwohl, curator at the Smithsonian Institution, Washington, D.C., and Gene Feldman, an oceanographer at the NASA Goddard Space Flight Center, Greenbelt, Md., present a case study of "Ocean Planet," a traveling exhibition that became "Ocean Planet Online." They vividly illustrate the process and implications of changing venues from a physical public space to the virtual world of the Web.

In their essays, Scott Sayre, director of print and electronic media at the Minneapolis Institute of Art, and Jay A. Levenson, director of the international program at the Museum of Modern Art, New York, direct our focus back to the program on the screen. Jay explores the issue of authenticity, recalling the long-standing debate over the value of reproductions, whether 35mm slides or digital files. Scott voices a caution that might be applied to any museum program developed for public consumption: Today's cutting-edge tool is tomorrow's scrap heap. He writes: "The most common reason for

. . . replacement results from changing visitor expectations." Speaking from the very practical and cost-conscious perspective of a developer, Scott reinforces Ruth Perlin's remark that "new technologies are not ends in themselves." Instead, he writes, "No matter how tempting the emerging technologies may be, the primary criteria for making investment and design decisions should always be determined by the technologies' ability to achieve a discrete set of formally defined objectives."

Those comments, together with the provocative essays by Steve Borysewicz, former exhibit developer at the Field Museum, and Kris Morrissey, curator of interpretation at Michigan State University Museum, East Lansing, and Doug Worts, educator/evaluator at the Art Gallery of Ontario, Toronto, make a clear and compelling statement: While we are addressing the issue of media, we are not talking about technology. Rather, we are talking about content, presentation, and institutional mission. We are re-evaluating the relationships between ourselves and our audiences, and between our collections and our audiences.

Elsewhere in this book, I address my own pet theme, the museum as media workshop. In an age where most of our information is derived from electronic media, whether the Internet, television, or video games, it is imperative that we develop better skills to read this media. From my perspective as a filmmaker, it is also imperative that we develop the skills to more effectively produce it. In our popular culture we have allowed television to define the terms of visual literacy. Television is a powerful and invasive tool, available in our homes 24 hours a day. Moreover, it is a tool that has been developed over a period of 50 years, ancient history to electronic media. It seems to me that museums have the authority—one might say the responsibility—to challenge this hegemony, to develop additional terms and examples, to provide new yet compelling visual information for our growing publics. If we want visitors who are critical thinkers, visitors who continue to appreciate the value of our collections, we must help them become more visually literate and teach them to become more accomplished consumers of the media that confronts them, both inside the museum and outside our walls.

chapter 1

Mediated Realities: A Media Perspective

Selma Thomas

Several years ago, I was standing in front of a video monitor in the lobby of the Smithsonian's National Museum of American History (NMAH), watching an animated interactive version of "Goldilocks and the Three Bears." This program was part of the museum's permanent exhibition "A Material World," and was designed to demonstrate materials testing: Goldilocks moves from one chair to another, from one bed to another, until she finds the perfect fit. I was standing with Tom Tearman, the museum's chief of exhibits, audiovisuals, and services, watching visitors interact with the program. We observed, with no surprise, as a young girl, about 9 years old, approached the screen. Goldilocks was just about to test Baby Bear's chair when the girl's mother pulled her away from the screen, reminding her (and us) why they had come to NMAH: "This is a museum. We did not come here to watch cartoons." Even as we laughed, Tom and I were chastened, perhaps more so than the girl who was being dragged off in search of culture. This was a vivid reminder of the status of media within the museum, even in the eyes of the visitor.

Media does not bring visitors to the museum. If they want to watch a movie, visitors will go to a movie theater. If they want to play a game, they will go to a video arcade. If they want a total immersion experience, they will visit a theme park. Why then do they come to the museum? The traditional answer is that they have come in search of "things"—real artifacts, real works of art, real objects. The museum exhibition displays and interprets these items. Increasingly, that interpretation has come to rely on some form of media.

Museums have always helped their visitors appreciate the value of objects, primarily by facilitating a direct encounter between visitor and object. New tools make possible new relationships and new insights. In the late 1980s, electronic media was embraced as a convenient and cost-effective tool. To some museums, media offered the means of contextualizing the object. To others, it promised greater audience appeal. For me, a historian turned filmmaker, the possibility of practicing one's craft inside the museum exhibition seemed like the perfect blending of form and function.

That is not to say that those early years of the 1980s were easy. Curators eager to use media, especially interactive media, might have to plead their case with a museum director suspicious of the high cost and low content. Alternately, directors, thinking it would draw younger visitors, might insist to a reluctant curator that interactive media (and its unplanned cost) be added to an exhibition already underway. In either case, the media producer often found herself working under adverse conditions, openly confronted by a hostile curator or a suspicious director.

Fortunately, that all-too-frequent suspicion made sense to me. As a museum visitor and a historian, I can appreciate the value and appeal of objects. As a filmmaker, I recognize the parameters that the museum exhibition imposes on media, in any format. When we produce media for theatrical presentation (whether as film or as television), we want the audience to suspend judgment and enter the world we have created on screen. When we produce media for museums, we hope to create a world on screen that is, likewise, real. But we don't want our audiences to suspend judgment, and we recognize that the reality we create on screen is surrounded by three-dimensional realities of artifact and space. These conditions impose strict conceptual demands on producers, forcing us to define clear and candid roles for the programs we create.

In some ways, the use of media inside the museum, especially the museum exhibition, would seem to violate the nature of the institution. If we believe in the primacy of the artifact, if we seek to interpret history, science, and art through the objects that each of these disciplines has created and collected, how can we justify the use of a mediated representation of these objects? As a museum visitor, why should I look at pictures of the object when I can walk into a gallery and see, for example, a real lunar rock, collected by an American astronaut and brought back to Earth?

That is not a question that we want the visitor to ask, but it is a question that the producer must ask before she begins any media project. The answers will inform both the conceptual and the technical approach to the electronic program. They will vary according to the parameters of the project, which include budget, schedule, content, audience, and venue, as well as institutional mission. Asking the questions "Why are we using media?" and "What do we hope to accomplish by using it?" raises more profound questions about the nature of learning and the limits and/or promise of visual language. We might ask: "What is the information that is best conveyed in words (text labels), in images (representations of 'real' artifacts), and in the reality-based object? How do we discover that information as scholars and museum educators, and how do we shape it as curators and media producers?"

Reality and Resolution

When I began work on this book I went back to the various papers I've written about "new media" over the past few years, thinking that my own position on the subject hadn't changed much since I began working inside museums. I was surprised to see how out-of-date some of these papers are. Some, less than 5 years old, refer to technologies that are now obsolete. That didn't surprise me. Rather, I was struck by how much more sophisticated the discussion has become in only a few years and by the degree to which my own position has shifted, though the early arguments are still discernible.

Those early papers stress the need for both content development and production value, that is, intellectual and aesthetic standards. Rob Semper, a contributor to this book, expressed the debate more elegantly at the 1996 American Association of Museums Annual Meeting in Minneapolis when he asked, "Is reality only a matter of resolution?" Rob's remarks were a private joke, since he and I have argued often, if amiably, about the need to instill our images with high production values. As a filmmaker, I may have a vested interest in those values, but I have come around to Rob's way of thinking. The value of our images is less literal than conceptual. It is that conceptual meaning that guides us, as producers and consumers of media. In other words, the technology is (or should be) seamless, providing a convenient means of serving an idea. Those attributes of convenience and of transparency are essential. The best media is integrated, architecturally and conceptually, into an overall exhibition narrative. Because it is an integral part of the exhibition, it must work all day, every day. To create a foolproof technology, the producer must understand the nature and capacities of the institution.

The conceptual purpose of media is realized by a combination of technical decisions: What is the most appropriate delivery system for this information? Do we have a budget that can support this technology, or will the budget force us to re-think our intentions, both conceptual and technical? Technology is inflexible. It will impose unchanging rules on the players. Like all rules, they must be learned and addressed, even when we choose to ignore them. One of the insights that hasn't changed over the years is the understanding that the pragmatic aspects of a technology must be addressed simultaneously with the conceptual development of the media. If the technology is the vehicle with which the concept is realized, the delivery system must be present and working all day, every day, or the interpretive program will be incomplete.

Form and Function

One could describe effective media programs by borrowing a list of clichés from other design arts. Like film, media in the museum is a collaborative art. Like architecture, the function of the program can be read in its form. If we cannot quote comfortably Ludwig Mies van der Rohe that "God is in the details," we can at least apply his unrelenting attention to detail to serve the same conceptual purpose.

There are two ways to look at media. First, one must look at media from the outside as one of many tools available to the exhibit developer. Why are we using it? How does it meet the museum's needs? What does it add to the broader educational lessons that will be addressed by other interpretive programs? Once we have identified an intellectual need, then we can begin to design the program to fill that need. But since these are labor-intensive technologies supported by expensive equipment, we must address also the institutional commitment and/or capacity to install and maintain the technology. If we want it to work every day, all day long, we cannot overestimate the level of commitment—time, effort, and money—that media will require of an institution.

But there is a second way to look at media and multimedia, and that is internally, judging them—technically, aesthetically, conceptually—as visual interpretive programs. Electronic media is image-based, and one might argue that there is serious content and first-hand information in images. How do we represent these images? In which format? How does the chosen format relate to other museum elements, to artifacts and/or exhibition design (if they are used in an exhibition)? What subtext does it impose on the information, on the images? How do we change the meaning of the image when we crop it to the ratio aspect of the selected format? In the interfaces that introduce computer programs to visitors, in the composition of individual frames (which sometimes force us to crop images), more obviously in the arrangement of frames and moving picture, we add layers of commentary.

The laserdisc project *American Art from the National Gallery of Art* (1993), produced by Ruth Perlin, converted transparencies to digital files to create an image bank of the National Gallery of Art's (NGA) American collection. The educational need was clear: to serve NGA's many distant publics, in the nation's schools primarily, by publishing a significant and popular collection. At a time when other producers were using digital technologies to create CD-ROM titles, Ruth knew her target audience well, and instead chose videodisc as her platform. She recognized the equipment limits and she understood the varied educational needs of her primary audience. In the early 1990s, American schools did not have the equipment to use CD-ROM technology. Art teachers who wanted access to high-quality pictures of the museum's American collection, to create their own lectures or to assign research projects to students, found the NGA laserdisc a flexible program. It provides several chapters, including: a brief introduction to the collection, narrated by the museum director, Earl A. "Rusty" Powell, and an image bank that reflects NGA's own cataloguing system, "Painting," "Sculpture," "Graphics," etc. Each work of art is represented by a title page with standard catalogue entries (artist name, dates, title, dimensions, medium) and by a full-frame image.

Larger, more complicated works are complemented by close-up details. A landscape, for example, will be represented by a full-frame, but the next frame might feature a detail of a leaf or the sky. The interpretive material is off-screen, in a hypercard stack that may or may not be used, depending on the individual teacher's lesson plan. Alternatively, the teacher might assign a group of students to write their own program/hypercard stack, based on additional assigned readings. A technology-shy teacher or student can make use of a barcode wand, since the package also includes a barcode guide. None of the technologies used was so state-of-the-art that it would become dated. Instead, they were designed to support multiple levels of inquiry for a long period of time.

If the producer's first task is to identify the educational message and the conditions under which that message will be delivered, her second task is to design a world on screen that is, if not "real," at least honest. Creating that world requires the concerted efforts of many participants, including producer, curator, and other museum professionals, as well as a host of technicians and artists (camera operator, editor, composer). Each of the participants brings to the project a combination of artistic and technical skills, and each skill must be managed to serve the central concept, so that no one of them will overwhelm the idea they all serve. When the project is complete, none of the independent tasks will be apparent to the viewer.

In traditional media, we expect an audience that sits, with little distraction, in a movie theater, in front of a television set, at a computer screen. The museum environment introduces competing distractions, including real objects and real people. The tangible realities of a museum exhibition—the architecture, objects, and audience—force producers to analyze the screen more judiciously. Why am I asking visitors to look at pictures of something? Why should they care about what happens on screen? What can I do to make them care?

Asking these questions forces us to analyze the nature of media, to learn what stories it can tell best and which it fails to tell. Addressing these issues in my work, I have learned to speak more directly to my audience and to consider the circumstances, both social and physical, in which that audience will watch the screen. At its best, the media that we create for museums helps us to achieve a dialogue between audience and text, whether that text is visual, written, three-dimensional, or simply implied in the broader narrative created by a careful arrangement of media, text, and object.

Media and Authenticity

The question of authenticity is central to everything we do in museums. It is what draws our visitors. It is what drives our quest for provenance and conservation, informing the selections we make for exhibition. In history museums the artifacts are generally three-dimensional—for example, Abraham Lincoln's top hat and Jacqueline Kennedy's Inaugural gown, two items selected for display in the traveling exhibition "America's Smithsonian" (1996-1997). It is, indeed, this associative value that makes history museums unique. Neither we nor our visitors appreciate these objects solely on aesthetic terms. Rather, we value them because of their connections to historical events or individuals, and we use media to make those connections.

But history museums also have collected music sheets from a young Duke Ellington, an early draft of the United States Constitution, a copy of Executive Order 9066, which justified the internment of Japanese Americans during World War II. These are pieces of paper, flat documents that we think don't have enough resonance to engage visitors on their own. So we produce a film or a video, or an interactive program, to make these paper artifacts come alive. For an exhibit on World War II, we want to recreate the simultaneous optimism and anxiety of that era, so we incorporate archival films into the show—Rosie the Riveter, for example, to illustrate the changing work force of the time. We tell ourselves and our visitors that archival film is another kind of artifact, one on which we will rely increasingly for the history of the 20th century.

In the company of authentic objects arranged in a physical narrative on race relations in ante-bellum Virginia ("Shared Spaces, Separate Lives," the Valentine Museum), how can I create a program with the same integrity? The interactive video program in "Shared Spaces, Separate Lives" invites visitors to investigate different historical documents (wills, petitions, letters) to gain access to personal accounts by African Americans living under slavery. These are authentic historical documents, but they are also inanimate records of personal anguish. Is it more "real" to hang the actual document behind a glass case or to ask actors to read them in voices and accents that suggest the emotional cost of this history?

Art museums invite their visitors to establish a different kind of relationship to the works on display, one that appreciates them for their aesthetic value. A representation of *La Danse* by Henri Matisse does not approximate the impact of the real painting. But the National Gallery of Art produced a video for the traveling exhibition "Great French Paintings from The Barnes Foundation." This video, *An American Collector* (1993), portrays *La Danse* (among many other works of art) in situ. It was produced to illustrate the singular principles of Dr. Barnes, as well as the idiosyncratic gallery he founded. In lieu of a visit to that gallery, the National Gallery's visitors could watch the video. A CD-ROM, *A Passion for Art: Renoir, Cézanne, Matisse and Dr. Barnes*, produced by Corbis Corporation, reproduces major works in the collection, allowing users to explore them close-up. The program also provides significant contextual information in lectures by noted art historians.

Neither the exhibition video nor the CD-ROM pretends to match the splendor of the original work of art. Rather, they use it in a visual reference. In both cases, that visual reference is as good as the technology allows. These are two educational programs that make use of different delivery systems to serve different intellectual goals and different audiences. Both programs have mediated the relationship between audience and art. But in different ways, both installations also altered the relationship between visitor and object. The clear distinction between the original Barnes Collection and the National Gallery's exhibition reminds us that the physical space of the actual exhibition imposes an organizing narrative on works of art. The exhibition becomes a kind of cultural artifact, one that alters, or mediates, the relationship between visitor and object. Electronic media may be a more candid recognition of the curatorial hand and the designer's influence at work.

Process and Product

It is the producer's task to respect the nature and integrity of exhibit artifacts and exhibition spaces while creating interpretive programs and installing technology into the exhibition. That task forces two distinct perspectives on the producer. First, we must be attentive to process, an aspect that is external to the actual screen content (which addresses the physical/architectural aspects of the media installation). Second, we must create an interpretive program. We are responsible for what happens on the screen, for creating a visual language that is spoken by us and read by our publics.

Language is a communal exercise and we don't invent it, no matter how innovative we are. We may invent the vocabulary of that language, in the images that we produce, but those images are arranged in a grammar that is recognizable to our readers. The structure of that grammar is determined, to a great extent, by the limits of the format we have selected. It is likewise enhanced by the conventions that each format has developed, which is why an understanding of popular culture is so critical to media. In other words, there are existing guidelines to help us develop and evaluate electronic media.

Several years ago, I received a phone call from a woman who works for a large government agency that develops exhibits, both permanent installations and traveling shows. Working in the office of public relations, she was given the task of writing both a script and an RFP (request for proposal) for an interactive interpretive program. Looking for advice, she had apparently called around several offices, and by the time she got to me she was more confused than when she started.

She wanted to know "How do I write a script for an interactive program?" In attempting to answer that question, both colleagues and outside contacts asked about authoring systems, flowcharts, storyboards, and hardware. These are the wrong questions to ask at the beginning of a media program.

If your exhibit calls for a glass case filled with telephones you don't need to build the case yourself. You define the parameters. How many telephones will it house? Where in the exhibit space will it go? How much space is allocated? What is the preferred or appropriate material? How big are the items that will be displayed? What are their aesthetic and conservation needs?

The answers to these questions will inform the designer and fabricator who will bring expertise to the task. But the task will have been defined by a curator (or exhibit developer), by someone we might call "the content expert." Like the traditional display case, the interpretive program that relies on electronic technologies must also start with a good idea. That imperative may indeed be stronger with media because—unless it serves a conceptual purpose—it can become dated and even obsolete. The media in "A More Perfect Union: Japanese Americans and the U.S. Constitution," at the National Museum of American History, was installed in 1987, yet it has never become out-of-date or old-fashioned, because it was designed and produced to serve an integral exhibition theme. The actual hardware is irrelevant, so long as it serves its original purpose—to support a program that the exhibition team defined.

The museum exhibition is a site-specific, social experience. Visitors, whether they come in groups or singly, expect to walk through a gallery following a narrative that is expressed by space and illustrated by objects. Visitors know that they are likely to encounter others in that space, and these encounters provide opportunities to further explore exhibition themes. This is a social experience, one based on real people, real places, and real objects. It is this reality that the media producer must acknowledge and address when designing a program for museum use.

Audience

If venue is a critical factor in shaping the external constraints of electronic media, then audience is the key influence on designing the program on screen. In 1994, the Smithsonian opened a temporary exhibition in Japan. "Smithsonian's America," under Project Director Lonnie Bunch, introduced American history and culture through the Smithsonian's collections. There were several electronic media throughout the exhibit and perhaps the most spectacular was a high-definition T.V. "music video" of Ray Charles singing his signature version of "America the Beautiful." This was a brief, three- to four-minute program with the song as the only narration. Visitors heard the soundtrack before they encountered the screen and there were many stories of visitors, American and Japanese alike, weeping in front of the large screen with its projections of American scenery, drawn from cities, small towns, and national parks around the country. The program was a powerful and emotional piece.

A year later, when the Smithsonian began to assemble the "America's Smithsonian" exhibition, which would travel to 12 American cities over a period of two years, Project Director J. Michael Carrigan wanted to use the same video at the beginning of the exhibition. When the exhibition team viewed the program, with an American audience in mind, we all cringed. It did not work for an American audience. In the first place, we had given prominence to Mt. Rushmore in the Japanese piece, since it is the single most popular tourist attraction for Japanese visitors to the United States. Although we found this information surprising, we knew that the site conveyed great meaning to our Japanese audience, and we included it in their version. To an American audience this was a baffling choice and we were forced to re-edit the entire program. The American version was both more and less literal: We illustrated amber waves of grain, purple mountains' majesty, sea to shining sea. We also included scenes from some of the cities to which the exhibition traveled, incorporating shots of a Los Angeles beach, a Houston skyline, a Detroit park. The song remained, though we added captions for an American audience (in compliance with the Americans with Disabilities Act). The images changed to address an American audience with a more intimate understanding of American life and culture.

The Children's Discovery Museum in San Jose, Calif., wanted a simple, linear video in "A Step into the Past," a permanent exhibit. The exhibit describes life in the Silicon Valley when it was still the Valley of Hearts' Delight, a productive agricultural community. Most of the museum's visitors, children and adults alike, are newcomers to the valley and few of them know the agricultural heritage of towns like Mountain View and Sunnyvale. The museum, like many children's museums, felt that interactive media would be treated as a toy and therefore would interfere with the educational goals of the exhibit. Instead, the museum preferred a simple program that might suggest a storytelling tradition: five individuals talk about their childhood growing up on farms in the Valley of Hearts' Delight. The program unfolds somewhat like a storybook with chapter headings that are both visual and spoken. A child narrator asks: "Did you have toys?" and the question is reinforced on the screen, in a still frame that depicts two stick-figured children under a golden sun. That chapter heading cuts to a former child, now a 70-year-old man, as he chuckles: "Toys? Well, we had teddy bears. But then most of our toys were something you could build, like blocks, and that's how you got your ABCs."

The camera is restrained, permitting the informants to move within a static frame. The graphics (chapter headings) appear to be simple and artless but they are the work of a sophisticated artist, one who has studied how children draw. When asked to draw a straight line, for example, children often take their pencil, draw part of a line, pull the pencil off the paper to check their progress, draw another section, review it, and continue in the same manner until they have a line, composed of several short lines, with discernible starts and stops. When children draw a sun, it invariably has rays, much like Picasso's sun. In creating the graphics for this program, we adopted the methodology of our primary audience. The roof line of our farmhouse is uneven. To illustrate the questions, we used the same black font that is familiar to our secondary audience (the adults who accompany children to museums). A quick reference to the "Dick and Jane" primers guided our selection of fonts. The narrator (who speaks the written questions) was a matter of great debate. We were told that the children who visit the museum ranged in age from 3 to 13. Our first inclination was to select a child from the middle range, aged 8. But we chose a 12-year-old narrator after we considered the "politics" of childhood. A younger narrator would be dismissed by the oldest segment of the audience, whereas an older voice would carry authority to the youngest visitors.

Multimedia

Few museum visitors know the difference between a television screen and a computer monitor, and the best electronic programs make the distinction irrelevant to the user. Instead, they present an immediate invitation to participate in an exploration, to move behind the screen into the seamless reality of another world. And that is the much more interesting problem, to create that seamless reality.

Everything we say about traditional electronic programs is true of multimedia programs. To serve museum needs they must address the specifics of venue and audience. They must be designed to support conceptual and aesthetic standards, and they must work all the time. While these programs will require more machine time, they are no more complicated than other projects, and in fact they are less interactive than most museum programs.

The effective multimedia program depends on many hours of programming. While it invites users to travel different paths of inquiry, the user can follow only a path that has been designed, produced, and programmed—which is to say that the editorial hand and eye of the producer is implicit rather than explicit. Who is responsible for the programming? In many cases, museums have yielded that task to computer specialists, as though computer activity equaled educational content. The result is often a cacophony of sights and sounds moving across the screen with no clear narrative. Technology can be intimidating, particularly since it seems to change, if not day by day, at least year by year. But the rate of innovation can also be liberating. Do we care which technology we select for a specific project, or do we care that it serve the program needs?

Multimedia forces on the producer a keen awareness of the audience. It makes us question the relationships between audience and us, between audience and artifact, between museum and the outside world. Done well, new media can redefine our relationship to the audience. It forces us to deal with the visitor's expectations—to reckon with the fact that the museum visitor must share our vocabulary, both visual and intellectual. Electronic media invites the visitor to participate in a transparent interface, and that invitation must be clear, direct, and logical. This requires a careful coordination of conceptual, technical, and design efforts. That coordination is familiar to anyone who works in public programs, and it can't be relinquished when those programs depend on computer technologies.

The best programs make the technology seamless. Our job is not to profile the technology. Our job is to express ideas, to interpret the information that is inherent in images (whether those images represent paintings or airplanes). This puts a great burden on the quality and content of the image. The technology makes available to the user information that is not resident in either the image or the object it represents. But it also allows us to refer to, indeed borrow from, the information that is resident in both. Multimedia gives us the means of adding and subtracting layers of commentary: It lets us and our audiences deconstruct both the information inherent in images and the nature of that information.

Image Content

When we discuss images, we say that they are powerful, emotional, gripping. It is this emotional quality that appeals to producers and audience alike. When we create images or borrow them from archival sources, we often choose them on the basis of their emotional impact. As producers and consumers of images, we employ and sometimes invent a visual vocabulary that allows us to explore ideas and methodologies that are not completely expressed in words. We tell each other stories, in historical programs; we examine works of art; we illustrate scientific processes—with images. If we want our audience to accept the veracity of these stories, the integrity of works of art, the credibility of process, then we must create images that are equally credible.

If we believe in the power of the primary source, how do we create programs whose integrity is equal to that of the surrounding artifacts, whether historical objects or works of art? That is the essential question of any program we might design for museum use. Any attempt to answer it will force the museum professional to address broader questions regarding the value of objects and the narratives that are, and are not, present in those objects. But it is a question that we might ask of other media as well. We have come to accept, even prize, the exhibition catalogue. Is the printed image more "real" than the electronic image? Certainly it is more familiar. Moreover, we associate the printed image with the printed word: This is a scholarly product, we tell ourselves. We associate the electronic image with television, a vulgar medium, one that doesn't typically support serious intellectual inquiry.

To accept such an assessment of media is to absolve it (and ourselves) from applying serious intellectual rigor to image-capture. Electronic images are a medium based on a visual vocabulary. To be effective, the vocabulary must be clear, logical, and direct, forcing us (as producers) to analyze each image. What is the intellectual content of the image, and what does that content illustrate and/or express? What is the technical content of the image; does it support or undermine the intellectual content? Aesthetic content is more difficult to define, since it is often culturally based, but one can create and apply standards.

The production of a media program is analogous to a

research project. Like any such project, it presumes a sequence of editorial decisions. Those decisions can be good or bad, well considered or shallowly conceived. The resulting images can be descriptive and expressive, or they can be banal and irrelevant. "What is this program about?" might be the first question, but the next is "What are the resources available to me?" Those resources, measured in time and money, will define the scope of the inquiry. But like any research project, the media program is only as good as the ideas on which it is based, since they will guide all technical, aesthetic, and conceptual decisions.

Image Capture

If the creation of a media program is a research project, the first step in the project is to select images, either from archival collections or from new footage. This critical step will determine not just what is included in the final program, but more importantly, what is not included. Images do us no good until they are in our hands and the lapse time between when we first see them, if they are published, or imagine them, if they are still to be shot, is fraught with mishap. At every turn, there are surprises. The producer must respond to each surprise while keeping in mind the original vision, a vision that must eventually take shape in front of multiple set of eyes. The eventual acquisition of archival images is both costly and time-consuming.

While you can't see the final program until it's finished, you can see clues along the way: a rough cut, a fine cut, a storyboard, a prototype. Not every image that we acquire will show up in the final piece, but the more and better images we acquire, the more informed, more effective is our final selection. Much like the notes one assembles in writing a book, the images that are assembled for an electronic publication must be studied. They will be employed in the creation of a rough draft, and they will become the basis of a final draft. Eventually, that draft will be "published" in a format appropriate to the final venue. The series of editorial decisions that drive the project will continue into installation, forcing a rigorous analysis at each of these stages. The objective of this exercise is a seamless narrative, one in which the technology disappears and the screen speaks directly to the audience in a candid, visual language.

The Museum as Media Workshop

Museums occupy fixed geographic addresses. They define real spaces, real galleries inside their walls. This is what draws visitors to museums. They come to see real artifacts. They want to see a painting by Leonardo da Vinci. They want to see the bed in which Abraham Lincoln died. These objects resonate deeply into our collective consciousness. Their physical presence lends their adjacent space significant cultural meaning. That connection to reality, that promise of authenticity, endows the museum with great authority, and it is an authority that we can borrow when we produce electronic media programs. This conceptual link to real collections lends to the electronic program both substance and authority. This connection clearly serves the museum's traditional goals to conserve and interpret real collections.

Producing media for museum exhibitions, I have come to appreciate the museum as a unique kind of media workshop. Unlike more celebrated media labs that experiment with technology to learn the limits of technology, the museum asks a media producer to explore the nature of learning. Broadcast television, which has sponsored many great films, imposes on media an unbending set of conventions. Broadcast pieces are narrated. They are cut to fill a pre-existing time slot. They are produced according to specific technical standards, so that they can be "broadcast" across a network.

Museums are closed technical systems. If they want to experiment with a new standard—high-definition T.V. for example—they can adopt the standard. If they want to install a computer system that allows users to zoom into extreme close-ups of old manuscripts, they can do so. If a three-minute video can weave an effective and complete narrative, the museum will use it, rather than insist on a program that is precisely 28 minutes and 30 seconds long. The museum world promises great intellectual, artistic, and technical freedom to the media producer.

The Lessons Learned

Museums also offer unparalleled opportunities to learn from the world's richest cultural institutions. From history museums I have learned to reveal the emotional information that is present in paper artifacts and to revive the contextual past of three-dimensional objects. From art museums I have learned to protect the aesthetic standards of a work of art, not by reproduction but by representation. We change the way that audiences read an image when we crop it, when we render it to a generic aspect ratio or a constant luminance. If we can't change the nature of the machine that depicts these images, we can refer to the limits imposed by the machine. Science museums have taught me to explore process and relationships, to give form and shape to ideas. Children's museums have taught me to study the way specific audiences learn. They have taught me to distinguish between primary and secondary audiences, and they have reminded me of the value of restraint. The Americans with Disabilities Act has forced me to consider all audience needs. Incorporating captions into a program, especially a multimedia program, invokes the primacy of text over image. These are lessons that one does not learn in film school or in traditional documentary work. They are lessons that might enhance any program in any medium. More significantly, they are lessons that might help us and our public develop the critical skills of media literacy.

chapter 2

Media and Museums:
A Museum Perspective

Ann Mintz

$]$t has become a truism that we've left the Age of Manufacturing and entered the Age of Information. The increasing use of computers to create, manage, and integrate very large databases and link people and information in real time raises interesting questions with enormous implications for the future.

The explosive development of information technology is transforming our lives in a variety of ways, large and small. Since the invention of the automated teller machine, "banker's hours" no longer mean anything; banking has become a 24-hour business. The developed world is moving toward a largely cashless economy based on global credit transfer and debit cards that pay for purchases with funds from personal bank accounts. Smart appliances turn the home kitchen into a technology showcase. Business people use video teleconferencing to conduct large-scale meetings without having to travel. Distance learning is now standard practice in schools across the country, with students learning Japanese, quantum mechanics, or non-computational algebra, live and in real time, from expert teachers who can be based anywhere there's a satellite uplink, high bandwidth Internet connection, or video-teleconferencing equipment. City kids make video field trips to museums and theme parks, and visit scientific expeditions from the Galapagos Islands to the bottom

Ann Mintz is executive director of the Science Center, Whitaker Center for Science and the Arts, Harrisburg, Pa., and chair of AAM's Standing Professional Committee for Media and Technology (1996-1998). This chapter is dedicated "to my husband, Clifford Wagner, and to Joel N. Bloom, with infinite thanks for his wisdom, his faith in me, and his friendship."

of the Mediterranean Sea. Teachers participate in hands-on science workshops developed by science museums located hundreds or even thousands of miles away.

Media and Museums

The Age of Information raises especially interesting issues for museums. On the one hand, museums are part of the information economy. By the current definition, museum professionals are "knowledge workers," engaged in the creation and transfer of information. On the other hand, it's a very special kind of information, based not on pure data but on real things.

Thus there is a paradox at the heart of the relationship between museums and computers. Computers can expand, deepen, and enhance the museum experience in a variety of ways. Yet in their very essence, museums are centered in the real world, on the collection, conservation, and interpretation of real objects. One of the central challenges facing museums is to utilize information technology without giving up our core identity: to embrace the virtual without abandoning the real. Museums have responded to this challenge by seeking to develop media experiences that are authentic in their own right but do not aspire to the kind of authenticity that by definition cannot be mediated, but requires direct access to an object, not a depiction of an object.

Computer-mediated technologies can and do enhance the museum experience for visitors in a variety of ways, both qualitative and quantitative. There are at least three ways that museums use computers to support their public activities. Computers can operate quantitatively, providing more information than is otherwise possible. They can operate qualitatively, providing a different kind of information than would otherwise be possible. A third, less conceptually complex option: Museums can present computers in their own right, either as artifacts or in computer-mediated works of art.

The Quantitative Dimension

Using computer technology to provide more information than is otherwise possible can address a major challenge facing curators and exhibit developers. Museum professionals and subject-matter experts are naturally more interested in a given topic than the general public. It is all too tempting for educators to tell people more than they want to know. Yet research such as Marilyn Hood's pioneering work on the psychology of leisure-time decisions shows that most visitors seek an experience that is social as much as educational (Hood 1983, p. 50). They enjoy the opportunity for interaction with each other and with the museum. This experience has been described by urban sociologist William Whyte as "triangulation"—the three-way interaction that takes place among two people and an object.

Reading large amounts of text can be incompatible with a social interaction that is clearly important to many visitors. Visitors may read a relatively small percentage of the text in a given exhibit, and the more text there is, the less they will read. Admittedly, the question of the optimum amount of text in a museum exhibit is both complex and contradictory. Visitors may read more than is suggested by standard time and observation studies. People browse as they walk through a museum, often reading as they walk. Pauline McManus's work shows that one visitor may serve as the "designated reader" for a group (McManus 1989, p. 92).

However, regardless of how much text an average visitor reads, different segments of the heterogeneous audience that visits museums seek different amounts of information. Computer technology can help visitors control the amount of information they receive, depending on their interest in a topic, the time available for a given visit, and the nature of their group. A computer can serve the information needs of the few without overwhelming the majority. A small percentage of visitors may choose to utilize all the technological resources of a multi-layered computer application, but their experience of the real object may be deepened and enhanced as a result.

For a completely different reason, technology can increase the amount of information an average visitor will accept. The same people who spend 15 seconds with a text panel or a work of art will spend as much as 15 minutes with a computer. This may be because computers are still relatively new to museums. Some visitors do not have personal access to computers, and the very novelty of the equipment may keep them interested. Or the fact that computer stations often are a place to sit may increase the amount of time a visitor is willing to spend at one.

Computers have a major role to play in our increasingly diverse, pluralistic society. Some exhibits, such as the "Busytown" exhibit developed by the Oregon Museum of Science and Industry, are available in both English and Spanish. By law, all exhibits developed for Canadian museums are in English and French. Multimedia developed for some American national parks is presented in as many as four languages. However, this does not begin to address the extent of diversity in some American cities, where dozens of languages are spoken. Computers have enough storage capacity to provide information in the most prevalent of these many languages. Of course, before it can be stored, the information must first be designed. Culturally appropriate interpretation requires more than simple translation. In this case, computer technology makes multiple languages possible, not easy.

Information technology can enhance services for the visually impaired. Using large-print screens or synthesized sound, computers can direct the visually impaired to experiences that do not depend on visual acuity. Interactive, scaleable text displays can allow the visually impaired to select the type size they find easiest to read. Few museums have utilized technology for this purpose, but it seems an inevitable next step.

Current information is another quantitative enhancement electronic media can provide. Even interactive exhibits are a static medium. Once they are developed, designed, and installed, it is difficult to update them without costly, time-consuming redesign. Computer technology allows museums to present information that may be as timely as this morning's news. The Hall of Human Biology at the American Museum of Natural History includes an electronic newspaper designed to offer current information in a flexible multimedia format. The Franklin Institute Science Museum's museum-wide Unisystem offered science news in each of the 20 permanent exhibits. Project staff selected information from on-line news services and routed it to an appropriate exhibit station.

Information technology also can provide personalized experiences for museum visitors. One of the most ambitious of these efforts was developed for the U.S. Holocaust Memorial Museum in Washington, D.C. The original plan was to match each visitor with a demographically similar person who experienced the Holocaust. Visitors would receive an individually bar-coded introduction to the person with whom they were matched. The designers structured the museum sequentially, from beginning to end. In each exhibit area, visitors would use the bar-coded card to learn what was happening to this individual. The goal was to personalize something that is basically unimaginable; the amount of information required made it impossible to realize this concept without computer technology.

Although this ambitious design was technically feasible, it did not succeed operationally. Producing printed materials in large quantities is a significant logistical challenge. Printers simply could not keep up with the demand for this customized material, and the system could not serve the enormous audience attracted to this extraordinary museum.

The Qualitative Dimension

Information technology can provide qualitatively different kinds of experiences, creating a new context for more conventional exhibitry. One of the most effective ways to accomplish this is to invite people to enter a virtual world, to go somewhere they cannot otherwise go. This may involve full-scale virtual reality, demanding powerful computers as well as body interfaces such as "eyephones"—goggles containing miniature monitors and motion detectors that allow the computer to respond to head and eye movements—and "datagloves" that allow people to manipulate objects in the virtual world. Simpler, more affordable strategies rely on the imagination of visitors to build a bridge between a media experience, either linear or interactive, and an exhibit.

The possibilities are endless. The simplest concepts parallel early television's "You Are There," taking visitors on a voyage to the bottom of the sea, to the moon, or back in time. The next layer of complexity invites visitors not just to visit or view a different world, but to interact with it. *Earth Over Time*, a videodisc developed for the Interactive Video Science Consortium established by a group of science museums, offers a rich array of interactive experiences. Visitors can travel to the sea floor and use tools such as a virtual microscope to examine sea life. They can view an interactive newscast on beach erosion; "talk" to the residents of a beachfront community; use a touch-screen ballot to choose an anti-erosion strategy, then travel into the future to see the results of their choice. The same videodisc offers activities on plate tectonics, vulcanology, and earthquakes.

Sophisticated applications allow visitors to explore virtual environments. Instead of making selections and choosing options, they can interact seamlessly, moving in any direction, entering any space that they pass, stopping to use an array of virtual resources or ask questions of a "guide." One such environment is a virtual tour of the Middle Kingdom fort at Buhen in Upper Egypt, developed by Boston's Museum of Fine Arts. Buhen was flooded by the 20th-century Aswan High Dam; it can only be experienced in the virtual world. Buhen is a relatively simple site; more complex environments can also be programmed, allowing visits to cities, artists' studios, or any other sites about which detailed information can be obtained.

Ideally, the link between the virtual and the real is explicit. In the early 1980s, an interactive videodisc in the Michael Rockefeller Wing at the Metropolitan Museum of Art in New York presented turn-of-the-(last)-century footage of various native peoples, such as Edward Curtis's films of the Kwakiutl tribe of the Pacific Northwest. This glimpse into a lost world is fascinating, but no relationship was established between the exhibit and the videodisc. Artifacts depicted on film were not linked with objects in the exhibit. Because of this lost opportunity for synergy, visitors could not easily build the bridge between media and exhibit.

A more successful installation was produced by co-author Selma Thomas for a daring exhibit at the National Museum of American History. "A More Perfect Union" explores the internment of Japanese Americans during World War II. It juxtaposes excerpts from the Constitution with specific events that directly conflicted with constitutional rights. One of the most effective sections re-creates a room from the internment camp at Manzanos. The room is stark and simple, bare wood with a narrow cot. Visitors approach it from one side; harsh sun and desert landscape can be seen through a full-size door on the other side. Then a middle-aged Japanese-American man and his teenage daughter approach the door. The figures are full-length and life-sized. "Dad, did you really live here?" the girl asks, beginning one of five short "one-act plays" that take place in this doorway. The actor who portrays the father grew up in an internment camp, and the script is based in part on his personal experiences.

This linear, non-interactive installation remains one of the most effective uses of technology in the creation of context. This is especially noteworthy since it is 10 years old at the time of this publication. Technology has advanced enormously, but the installation stands on its own merits and is not at all dated.

A videodisc produced for the Oakland Museum of California employs a different strategy to bridge the gap between media and museum. Its goal is to use technology to encourage visitors to look closely at specific individual objects. Selections from the permanent collection are displayed on-screen wrapped in brown paper. A series of clues challenge visitors to identify the "mystery objects," which they can then find in the exhibits. The media sharpens their focus, helps them look more closely at a few objects rather than glance at many in a cursory fashion.

Storytelling is another appropriate use of media in museum exhibits. "KidsBridge," an exhibit on prejudice at The Children's Museum, Boston, uses media to convey first-person stories. A diverse group of real Boston teens tells stories of their own experiences with prejudice and recounts their emotional reactions. The San Jose Children's Museum invites children to interview seniors about their childhood experiences.

Museum projects do not always recognize the power of media to tell stories. The Getty Museum developed a videodisc about its magnificent collection of classical Greek red- and black-figure vases. The disc is technically superb, the production values impeccable. Yet the focus is entirely on the vases themselves, not on the stories they depict or the role they played in their original context. The project fulfilled its goals, which focused entirely on art history. Nevertheless, it was a lost opportunity to use the medium more effectively.

A subsequent Getty videodisc incorporates that kind of contextual information. It interprets medieval illuminated manuscripts, and allows visitors to learn more about the meaning, functions, and symbology of these windows into a distant world. Visitors can select short films that demonstrate techniques of medieval scribes, artists, and bookbinders; explain the symbolism that is often obscure to contemporary visitors; describe the manuscripts in the

Getty's collections; and provide in-depth information about five specific manuscripts.

Media is ideally suited to address a challenge that has become of particular interest to museums in recent years: to present multiple points of view on a single topic. The Computer Museum in Boston employed media for this purpose in a recent exhibit called "Networked Planet." Visitors can select one of four "guides" to mediate the exhibit for them. Some of the guides are transparently enthusiastic about new technologies; others have concerns about their implications. Visitors can select the guide whose point of view is most compatible with their own, or seek out contrasting opinions. The guides are diverse in age, gender, and ethnicity, providing more options for visitors and allowing most people to "find themselves" in a guide.

Museum use of media is in its infancy, and information technology offers many options that have yet to be realized. Imagine an art exhibit that includes the opportunity to learn more about an artist's style by experimentation with interactive multimedia. A visitor could select components to assemble a painting, experiment with color, shadow, and perspective. Existing software can "grab" a single frame of video and display it in any one of dozens of different styles. A visitor could choose or create a picture, and ask to see it in the style of Botticelli or Braque. She could compare the Braque-style version to a pseudo-Picasso or Duchamp, and learn about the differences in style and technique.

Few art museums would approach art so irreverently, but many explore the options that information technology presents. Most, such as the Micro Galleries at the National Galleries in London and Washington, D.C., are located in resource areas rather than in exhibitions. In the mid-1980s, the Art Gallery of Ontario [AGO] in Toronto employed a simple, low-end, black-and-white Macintosh in a gallery dedicated to the work of a group of Canadian painters known as the Group of Seven. Its goal was to help people view art from the perspective of the expert, and it provided a framework or a structure for exploration—what is known in educational psychology as "cognitive scaffolding."

Educational psychologists will tell you that it is easier to learn when previous knowledge creates an armature to which new knowledge can be attached. This is the intellectual equivalent of "the rich get richer." Experts do not simply know more than novices, they approach a topic differently. Computer-mediated technology can help visitors experience an exhibit more like an expert, in a more knowledgeable way. That is what AGO accomplished in its installation in the Group of Seven gallery. Technically very simple, it was conceptually quite sophisticated. Visitors were invited to compare and contrast paintings using specific criteria, from emotional content to color palette. They also could use the computers to find out more about the lives of the painters, and enter their own thoughts in an electronic comment book.

Modest though this project was from a technical standpoint, it succeeded in its primary goal: to encourage visitors to look at art more carefully. However, at least a few visitors were offended by the inclusion of technology in an art exhibit. One commented that such things belong in Disneyland, not in a museum—a heated response to a single, small black-and-white computer screen!

Computers as Computers

The third way museums use computers is straightforward: as computers. The Computer Museum, Boston, which is dedicated to computers and computing per se; science museums; science-technology centers; and children's museums offer exhibits that explore computers as a topic. They may focus on computers as artifacts, the history or social implications of computing, or current developments in information technology. Computer-mediated art may be presented in these museums, or in museums of contemporary art. Artists such as Paul DeMarinis and Ed Tannenbaum have produced notable work under the auspices of the well-known artists-in-residence program at San Francisco's Exploratorium. This is the least complicated and the most "museum-y" use of computing in museums. In this context, the virtual quite literally is the real.

What's Different about Museum Media

Museums are educational institutions, and many educational programs have been developed for home, school, and library computers.

It seems logical that these programs could be placed in museums. However, this does not mean that a program developed for these markets will meet museum needs. Museum media differs from applications developed for other venues in at least four aspects.

The first is context. An application in a museum exhibit does not stand alone. It supplements elements as diverse as paintings, ethnographic collections, dinosaur skeletons, interactive mechanical devices, or entire rooms. As discussed above, a museum media program is most effective if it complements other aspects of the exhibit in which it is placed. It is further strengthened if it explicitly refers to its surroundings.

Museum visitors vary in age, education, interests, and learning styles. Some choose to focus on electronic media; others choose to ignore it. For many visitors, media can deepen and enhance other learning experiences.

In contrast, applications designed for use in homes, schools, or libraries must be entirely self-contained, independent from other components. This is not to say that an application developed for other uses cannot be placed in an exhibit, but it is unlikely to support the exhibit as fully as a custom production.

The physical context provided by the museum as a public space, the exhibit in its entirety, and spontaneous interaction with staff and other visitors are important parts of the museum experience. Media can deliver information; it cannot match the totality of the experience a museum provides. For this reason, a case can be made that there will never be a "virtual museum" in the full sense of the word. High-resolution images, full-scale virtual reality, and rich links to other databases on the World Wide Web do not create a museum. A virtual visit to a museum is fundamentally a media experience, not a museum experience.

Content is the second area where museum media differs from media developed for home use. Museum media exists, above all, for the purpose of educating the user. Computer games developed for an arcade or the home must be entertaining and challenging, but most productions developed for these markets have little educational content. Although it is true that these games can improve hand-eye coordination, it is difficult to make a convincing case that split-second reaction time is a significant educational goal.

User interface—how the user interacts with the equipment—is another area that presents special challenges to museums. How is the production started, stopped, interrupted? How does the user communicate with the program, and vice versa? A museum program must be easy to learn. The technology should be "transparent," interfering as little as possible with the experience. Visitors often "browse" in a museum, glancing at a display in a cursory manner and then moving on. There is a small window of time in which a visitor decides whether to pay closer attention or to move on. Because visitors become frustrated if they cannot learn to control a media program, the ideal interface must be understood quickly. Responsiveness is also important. It must be clear to visitors that their commands have been received by the computer and are being acted on. Visitors, especially adults, may be baffled by commands that are familiar to the computer literate. Even when commands are clear, unfriendly interfaces are surprisingly common. Command icons may be displayed in small print that is unreadable to older eyes or anyone with less-than-perfect vision. Manipulating a mouse or trackball may present other problems for the user.

As computers become more powerful, they offer more options and deeper opportunities for true interaction. Ironically, the sheer number of choices can easily complicate the development of a user-friendly interface. True virtual reality can provide a simple, all-but-seamless interface, but without extremely powerful computers, even a split-second delay in response time has been known to cause motion sickness in a sizeable minority of users!

Pattern of interaction is the final area in which museum programs present unique constraints. A museum application must attract and hold the visitor's attention in a rich, highly competitive visual environment. The window of opportunity to entice a visitor is measured in seconds, so the program should provide immediate satisfaction. Complex, multi-branched menus can offer too many choices. As a rule, visitors should reach their destination after making no more than three or four choices. Otherwise, they may become lost in the computer's changing screens or abandon the effort altogether. It also is important to allow people to change their minds and leave a selection before it is completed.

Museum media is rarely designed for extended interaction.

Many people visit museums in social groups, and are not well-served by experiences that preclude interaction with friends and family. Many museums serve large audiences. These museums have learned to consider "throughput," a concept defined by theme parks to describe the number of people who participate in an experience in a given unit of time. A good, short media experience serves more people and is more effective in meeting visitors' social needs.

Museums and Computing: The First 20 Years

As a medium, the museum exhibit is literally thousands of years old. (There were museums in Babylon in the first millennium B.C., and ancient Athens had the Pinakotheke, an art gallery on the Acropolis.) By comparison, museum computing is in its infancy. Yet research and experience lead to some conclusions that are unlikely to be rendered obsolete by technological developments.

1. Computers are not smart. People can use computers in intelligent ways, or less-than-intelligent ways. Throwing a computer at a problem won't fix it. Adding a computer to a boring exhibit produces a boring exhibit with a computer.

2. Computers are not necessarily the best way to serve children. Many museums justify the use of computers with the rationalization that it will give kids something to do. Ironically, many children's museums are very careful about how they use computers in exhibits, concerned about adding to the time that children already spend watching television and interacting with computers at home and at school.

3. The first question to ask is not "What can I do with a computer?" or "What kind of computer should I get?" but "What am I trying to accomplish?" The process must begin with the museum and its needs, and the first step is to define these needs. At this stage, knowledge about technology is needed primarily to establish what is possible.

4. The experience that technology delivers is much more important than the technology itself. Computers are ephemeral. Information technology develops at astonishing speed. Technical razzle-dazzle has a very short shelf life. This year's state-of-the-art is next year's blue-light special. A good experience is not rendered

obsolete by new technology. Any computer application must be able to stand on its own merits—the experience it delivers—rather than the technology that delivers the experience.

5. The technology itself can be distracting and intimidating. The most important thing is to learn to think intelligently about how to use information technology. Every profession has its guild secrets; in the computer business, these are expressed in letters and numbers. Unless you truly love the technical side of things, it isn't productive to start with the equipment, if only because it sets up the wrong power dynamic between the museum, its technical consultants, and its donors.

6. To be a satisfying part of the museum experience, computer and multimedia applications must be done well. Studies at the Media Lab at the Massachusetts Institute of Technology confirm that the average American is very sophisticated about electronic media. Thousands of hours of broadcast and cable television have taught us more than we realize. Top-of-the-line has established the norm; anything less looks shoddy, like cheap advertisements on late-night local TV.

Good production values are not inevitably expensive. Although very few museums can spend hundreds of thousands of dollars for each minute of on-screen programming, good design can be affordable. The first step is understanding the goals of the project. It is very difficult to fulfill a goal without knowing what it is. When the goals are clear, a variety of strategies can help produce affordable computer and multimedia applications. Satisfying computer animations can be created on personal computers; successful videodiscs have been produced for as little as $150.

7. Remember the visitor. Focusing on the visitor leads to a whole cascade of positive implications. Computer applications should be accessible to the whole range of museum visitors, including those who use wheelchairs. They must be durable and easy to operate, even for visitors with no computer experience. Children are rarely self-conscious about experimenting with computers in public places; adults often are. This is one reason to proceed with caution when installing large screens for secondary viewing. Adults hate to make mistakes in front of an audience, especially their own children.

8. Information technology in museum exhibits should be

used to expand visitors' options, not limit them. The Franklin Institute's Unisystem was originally designed to use cards that defined visitors as adults, children, or pre-schoolers and automatically provide programs designed for these groups. Mistake. Visitors hated it. They wanted to move freely between the programs, and resented the fact that the system made these decisions for them.

9. Designers of computer-mediated experiences bear a special responsibility. When visitors cannot use a computer successfully, they are more likely to conclude "I am not capable of doing this" than "This is poor design." Most people come to museums to enjoy themselves, not to feel self-conscious and stupid. It is counterproductive for an educational institution to send people away feeling less intelligent than when they arrived.

10. Evaluation is the only way to reality-check a project. It is a crucial part of the development process. It may extend the project time line, but in the long run, it is the most cost-effective strategy. Museum visitors may interpret a program very differently from the way the designers intended. An enormously expensive project can be compromised by flaws that could have been revealed by formative evaluation. Some applications are so counter-intuitive that visitors report them as broken when they are functioning perfectly.

11. Museums can become involved in complicated relationships with donors who want to provide computer technology. Sometimes this is the equivalent of remaindered goods—donors looking to write off material that didn't sell well. Conversely, a donor may want a museum to feature "the latest thing" to showcase their latest products. This creates its own complications. First-generation technology is not always very robust, and the bugs may not have been worked out yet. Unless the donor is willing to commit to a sustained presence, it is dangerous to teach the public to expect the latest thing— an expectation few museums can fulfill with their own resources. Stay focused on your own needs.

12. Computer people are an important part of the team, but they are not always the best team leaders. They may not be able to differentiate between a programming challenge that was fun to develop and an application that visitors enjoy using. A hypercard architecture that is transparent to a programmer may be incomprehensible to a visitor.

Some computer people are pathological optimists. In the face of all evidence, they tend to expect that everything will work perfectly. Phrase your questions carefully. Never ask, "Is it possible to do?" To some computer people, everything is possible. Ask how many people it will take, and how long. Ask if the technology they're recommending is currently on the market. This is, after all, the industry that invented the concept of "vaporware," technology that exists only in the nebulous zone between concept and marketplace.

13. Consider the operational implications of decisions about technology. Getting involved in computer-mediated technologies is like buying a house. The up-front costs—the down payment— are only part of the deal. The ongoing costs—the mortgage—must also be considered. Computer technology, both hardware and software, requires routine operational maintenance. Problems are likelier to occur on weekends, when public usage tends to be heaviest and staff support is most difficult to obtain.

14. Be realistic. Regardless of the preventive maintenance schedule, no computer application is as trouble-free as a painting or a natural history diorama.

The Virtual and the Real

In the developed world, more and more information is obtained vicariously, much of it through various electronic media. The museum experience is based on reality. This is the heart of the concept of museums. Monitors may be pleasantly hypnotic, but looking at a painting on a video screen is no substitute for the real thing. The real thing is more subtle, and more powerful. The reasons are both physical and metaphysical. On a video screen, a painting has no texture; something is always lost when three dimensions are collapsed into two. Distinctions of scale disappear; a tiny Renoir and a gigantic David are the same size. The electronic palette cannot perfectly match colors in the real world. The eye and brain process information from an object one way, and information from a monitor another way.

The metaphysical dimension is more difficult to describe, but it is very real. Many people—professionals and visitors—recount powerful personal experiences in museums. In 1994, the nonprofit research organization Science Learning, inc. (renamed Institute for Learning Innovation in January 1998), convened a group of museum professionals to discuss research on learning in museums. Participants from different disciplines described museums as the settings for what psychologist Abraham Maslow called "peak experiences." Virtually all included words such as "awe" to describe what can only be called epiphanies—transcendent, even life-changing experiences. All were based on experience with real objects. None of the 50 participants chose an experience with media or technology. Similarly, the participants in Michael Spock's videotaped interviews on pivotal learning experiences in museums recounted experiences with objects, visitors, and staff, not with information technology.

A *New York Times* review of the CD-ROM version of the London Micro Gallery observed that no matter how good the image quality, a computer takes art and turns it into cultural information. Information can be conveyed electronically. The enduring experience of art cannot.

Information technology is a means, not an end. It can enhance the experience of the real thing in wonderful, meaningful ways. It cannot replace it. These technologies have enormous potential, but it would be foolish indeed to choose exquisite simulations over direct experiences with reality. In this media-saturated world, the museum may be more important than ever.

References

Hood, Marilyn. 1983. Staying away: Why people choose not to visit museums. *Museum News* 61, no. 4: 50-57.

McManus, Pauline. 1989. Oh yes they do! How visitors read labels and interact with exhibit texts. *Curator* 32, no. 3.

chapter 3

Multimedia in Living Exhibits: Now and Then

Michael H. Robinson

Why has not man a microscopic eye?
For this plain reason, man is not a fly
                              —Alexander Pope (1733)

In a community where public services have failed to keep abreast
of private consumption things are very different. Here in an
atmosphere of private affluence and public squalor, the private
goods have full sway.
                              —John Kenneth Galbraith (1963)

Introduction

On the eve of the next millennium, there can be little doubt that the non-human part of the living world faces a major crisis of extinction, degradation, and constriction. The reasons for this crisis are embedded in the unprecedented and largely unpredicted expansion of human activities in the 20th century characterized as "The Age of Extremes" in a brilliant book by Eric Hobsbawm (1995). Whatever might have been the expectations for the future, as the bells rang on the eve of our times they probably did not anticipate a century of

Michael H. Robinson, director of the Smithsonian Institution's National Zoological Park, is an animal behaviorist and a tropical biologist. He is the author of more than 150 papers and articles, including a book on the courtship and mating behavior of spiders. A version of this chapter appeared in the July/August 1997 issue of Museum News.

"megadeaths" and "cornucopia economics" (Brzezinski 1995). The tripling of the human population, the 14-fold increase in the use of fossil fuels, and the gargantuan increase in the world economy by 29 times all speak to the causes of our present negative impact on the living world.

It is in this context that the informal education role of bioexhibits (zoos, aquariums, wildlife parks, aquariums, marine-lands, botanic gardens, arboretums, and natural history and anthro-pology museums) must be viewed. They have a crucial role to play in ensuring that there is a bioliterate world electorate. And since the task of education is now properly regarded as forging horizontal con-nections between fields of knowledge and scholarship, in addition to its conventional role of reinforcing vertical ones within these, bioex-hibit institutions must form links with all public exhibit institutions, museums, galleries, and the like. I have repeatedly stressed the need for a new interlocking and intertwining of the formerly isolated pro-grams within bioexhibitry and for the evolution of zoos (zoological parks) into bioparks (Robinson 1986-95). What, then, is the broad context of education for bioliteracy? How might institutions use mul-timedia approaches for this purpose, and how can they relate to the potentially, but not always actually, synergistic mass media of T.V., radio, film, and the information superhighway?

We can deal with what is in use now and speculate on the future then. If this context of biodiversity crisis appears apocalyptic or excessively hyperbolic, it may simply reflect my nearly 20 years of research and residence in the tropics. Even if future reality is less cat-astrophic, our knowledge of biology will be a decisive factor in wise-ly and successfully sustaining our planet's habitability. Before consid-ering the what and how of how multimedia is being used and how it will affect museums and bioexhibit institutions, it is worth briefly set-ting it in an historical context.

For the purposes of this essay I define multimedia presen-tations to include all forms of interconnected multisensory presenta-tions, including visual, auditory, tactile, kinesthetic, and olfactory experiences, whether developed through mechanical or electronic devices or by experiences of living organisms. The latter category is unique to living bioexhibits or live presentations mediated by humans.

History Communication

Essentially, education is communication—it involves at least two-way interactions. As a species our earliest communication was probably by face-to-face visual signals, reflecting optical dominance, and by extensive vocalizations as seen and heard in most primates. Each of these modalities has distinct adaptive advantages dependent on prevailing environmental factors. Social interactions in primates make use of multiple transmission media, and increasing intelligence makes possible the interpretation of contextual clues about meanings and reliability. When sounds are used in language a substantial and almost infinite potential for information transmission occurs. In human history, storytellers and other forms of oral transmission extended the generational life of orally transmitted information. Written language extended it even further and itself expanded audience accessibility by the invention of pens (think of writing with ink and illuminated manuscripts). Transmission increased with the invention of printing and, later, movable type. Like exhibit institutions, books evolved from the province of the wealthy to a virtual democracy, furthered by public free libraries and paperback books. Oral transmission requires the ability to hear, written transmission requires the ability to read. Even now, in the second half of our century this is not universal. Literacy is still patchily distributed; for instance, in 1981, only three African countries had an adult illiteracy level that was below 60 percent.

Newspapers were almost "instant books." And then cables increased the distances over which written language could be rapidly transmitted. This was followed by advances in oral transmission through predigital voices: telephony, radio, recordings. A further advance in non-written visual communication occurred with the invention of cinephotography, which was silent for at least a quarter of our times. Then came the "talkies," still a major means of mass communication in such less-developed countries as India. Then television dominated but did not entirely replace the movies in most industrial societies, and now extends into cable and satellite propagation, in addition to broadcast diffusion. Video taping and video-loan "libraries" have augmented further the audio-visual media audiences. CD-ROM technology, may be on the point of being miniaturized to the stage of portability and ultimate low cost. The e-mail revolution, apparently a mind-boggling expansion in truly interactive, distance-reducing communication, may, on its dark side, lead to the increasing withdrawal of humans from direct interpersonal social contacts, and reduce rich social interactions involving the plethora of sensory cues that are part of live person-to-person encounters.

History Audiences

In the ultimate sense museums, like most of our institutions, owe their origins to great events of barefoot biology that occurred in several centers around the world about 10,000 to 12,000 years ago. Then, after an almost interminable period of hunting/gathering, amounting to perhaps 99 percent of the existence of the genus *Homo*, we domesticated a handful of plant and animal species, freed ourselves from reliance on the natural and limited carrying capacity of our environment, and civilization came into existence. With it came the origin of cities, the division of labor, and the unequal division of wealth. Structured monarchic societies produced institutions that were protomuseums and restricted to privileged social groups. Zoos and botanic gardens originated in Imperial China and Pharonic Egypt at least 4,000 years ago. They were essentially royal collections of animals and plants and reflections of pomp and power. Pomp and power continued, for most of subsequent history, to be expressed in collections of objects ranging from art to "curiosities" that were accumulated in the centuries of pre-industrial civilization. Added to these were objects associated with religious reverence, often regarded as sacred, which overlapped the contents of protomuseums. Broad public access to the collections of the royal or wealthy was either nonexistent or sporadic. On the other hand many objects of reverence were more broadly accessible in cathedrals, churches, temples, shrines, and mosques.

This essentially non-inclusive period in the history of museums had its exceptions, but it was not until the Industrial Revolution that there was a growth of democratized museums. Of course there were still extensive private collections, as there are today. There was also a world division of national haves and have-nots. The largely northern colonial powers plundered the natural and cultural wealth of the poorer and subject nations and their art, artifacts, and flora and fauna. Cities that were centers of European colonialism sparkled with plundered treasures of antiquity (and still do). This collectionism also extended to alive or stuffed exotic animals that provided public spectacles at zoos and natural history museums in London, Paris, Berlin, New York, Washington, Rome, and so on. Public art collections paralleled the growth of such collections of curiosities.

Our century saw a further expansion of public exhibits in the developed world. In the United States, for instance, 95.5 percent of the existing 8,179 museums have been created since 1900 (AAM 1994). The figures for Europe are probably not as striking as these. The present state of U.S. museums is one of still accelerating efflorescence. According to the AAM survey, of the 8,179 museums in the United States, 75.5 percent were created in the second half of the 20th century! The proportions of different subject-classes of museums is interesting and, to me, counterintuitive. History museums preponderate at 29.4 percent, and if historic sites are added, amount to almost 55 percent of the total. Since most exhibited U.S. history is post-Columbian, this is very surprising. Art museums account for 14.8 percent, ranking second in categories, they also have by far the largest operating income. Natural history and anthropology museums account for a tiny 3.1 percent of the total, 2.4 percent less than the living plant and animal exhibits (zoos and botanic gardens).

This is a simplified and simplistic survey, but I think that there is sufficient truth in it to demonstrate that public access to what we are defining as museums is a recent phenomenon. (In concentrating on private and public spectacle I have ignored the research and scientific role of collecting, and the non-public storage of collections, as well as the "nation's attic" function of museums in preserving items from the present for the public of the future.) Even using the most generous interpretation, public access is perhaps a three-century-old phenomenon in the developed world. Clearly cultural institutions are now overwhelmingly open to the public; for educators, this has raised problems that are highly relevant to our subject. This is partly because there has been widespread access to non-institutionalized mass media, that has raised expectations and set standards of information transmission. There is, of course, a real-life distinction between freedom of access and practical accessibility.

History Function

Clearly there has been an evolutionary change of function parallel with that of audience composition. Regal or aristocratic pomp gave way to public spectacle that gradually acquired the adjuncts of explanation and exposition. Throughout the triumphant economic, and sometimes imperial expansion of northern industrial societies exhibits there were also celebrations. Almost without exception these celebrated "National Achievement"—always a capitalized subject. (The great Crystal Palace exhibits of Victoria's empire were celebrations of nationalistic collectionism as powerful as the triumph ceremonies of Imperial Rome. They included thinly disguised and sometimes blatant exhibits of subject peoples. Earlier, Napoleon's triumphal exhibitions of his booty and plunder paralleled his magnificently orchestrated triumphal marches or processions. And the purportedly internationalist U.S.S.R. had massive displays of the achievements of Soviet science, and Soviet agriculture.) This essentially patriotic mode has persisted far into our times. In recent years huge international expositions, so-called World Fairs, have consisted of pavilions celebrating National Achievements and pride, and have iconized competing ideologies. For all their disclaimers to the contrary, they have been expensive expressions of rivalry and "one-upmanship."

At a somewhat lesser pitch museums have functioned, to use an apt metaphor, as temples. For example, art galleries function as temples of a range of esthetics—classical, modern, contemporary, *ad extenso*. Recently this approach, and the purely celebratory, has been challenged. For instance, the publication of AAM's 1992 report, *Excellence and Equity: Education and the Public Dimension of Museums*, represented a coalescence of views that had been fermenting for a decade or more. The immediate result of this publication, and of the professional meetings that were organized around it, was a further national discussion on the nature of the public dimension of museums. The idea of the museum as a forum rapidly displaced the idea of the museum as a temple. Practice lags behind.

Problems in Visitor Education

Before proceeding I have to declare some biases. I am an evolutionary biologist whose research has mainly involved the study of animal behavior, and with this I am an incurable "biophiliac," to use a term coined by sociobiologist E. O. Wilson (1986). I believe that bioliteracy is essential for solving the problems both of our times and those predictable for the next millennium. Being an ethologist I have a prejudice for observing and experimenting with behavior and against using the survey methods of sociology and some branches of psychology. I am also an ex-schoolteacher and a maverick in my present profession for believing that the primary function of zoos and other bioexhibit institutions is education, not *ex situ* species conservation. (Of course I also believe that education is a primary function of all museums.) As an ex-researcher I am convinced that good exhibitions are based on good research and all museums should support excellence in research.

There are two themes to be aired. How do we educate, and how do we extend our audience to the broadest possible extent? The two themes are not easily separable, but I'll try to concentrate on the first issue of *how* rather than *who*. To define terms: I use museum as an all-inclusive word, definitely comprising all kinds of bioexhibit institutions.

The whys and hows of museum education are extremely complex. Having set them in their historical context, we also need to summarize present trends. The brief outline of the history of human communication, above, is relevant. For a growing number of people, the world of the 1990s is one in which the printed-word media are being replaced by ubiquitous television. By the age of 18, the average child in the United States is estimated to have watched more than 16,000 hours of television. This is more time than that spent at school (Falk and Dierking 1992). How much of that time is educational in any acceptable sense of the word? Books may become antiques, to be treasured by collectors, long before they are objects venerated by the Starship Enterprise's Captain Picard. Radio is alive and well, but flourishes less and less. Movies linger on, differently popular in a world where technology is patchily distributed. In the developed world, the present is overwhelmingly one of widespread computerdom and particularly of computer fluency among the young (children of the '70s, '80s, '90s). Even in rich societies there are disparities in access to computers based on social class, and places where social class reflects ethnicity to a greater or lesser extent. Interactive portable electronic multimedia devices will soon be commonplace, along with virtual reality. These changes have profound implications for museum attendance and exhibit-based informal education.

That said, how do we educate in museums? Educational theory advances, but it advances slowly, and the investment is pitifully small considering its importance. How to train troops in the techniques of their trade may get more attention and research investment than how to educate kids for the needs of a rich and satisfying life. Investment in advertising and marketing theories is rigorously tested in the societal/commercial struggle for existence, by direct measures of success, in a way that has never happened in the world of education. Advertising is a rigorous field that educators seem to consider "untouchable." Our biological/chemical understanding of how our brains work is a rapidly expanding field full of excitement, promise, wonder, and hints of important breakthroughs. Most of what we know speaks of the importance of motivation, curiosity, interest, or drives, as well as multiple factors that canalize learning. Redundancy, often translatable into multimedia or multiperceptual repetition, plays an important role.

As an evolutionary biologist, I am convinced that our young are programmed by past selective forces, hard-wired to absorb massive amounts of information and store them. The period when this happens is probably without major filters, and occurs in part before powers of information- or fact-weighing judgment and discrimination are developed. This is full of perils, most of which are real rather than potential (Dawkins 1995). Unless we provide some external filtration there is a strong possibility the mind will absorb junk. Our absorption of information occurs by way of several sensory modalities of which vision is crucially important. The balance of emphases varies among humans, so the present focus on providing for a variety of ways of learning makes sense. The addictiveness of some kinds of recurrent themes, images, and sounds, so effective in advertising and soap operas, is worthy of study. It would be interesting to discover the natural origin(s) of this propensity in our pre-civilized lifestyles. Clues to the biological nature and bases of powerful addiction to certain categories of perceptual experience could guide the design of our institution/collection-based educational methods. It would be nice to know what lies behind addictive fascination so we could exploit it.

Exhibiting Biology Interactively

At the National Zoo we have decided that an important aspect of our educational activities is to make interconnections between knowledge, and that a major problem with informal bioeducation has been the fragmentation of knowledge resulting from the Victorian academic climate that separated botany from zoology, and both of these from paleontology, anthropology, geology, geography, and other earth/life sciences. Within zoology itself there were further disciplinary separations that became reflected in institutions. Thus zoos exhibited living animals without reference to the history of life on Earth; the history of human interactions with life; crucial interactions with the plant kingdom; the inner structure of organisms; the relevance of animal biology to human biology; and so on.

We have suggested that the zoological park, or zoo, should evolve into a biological park, or biopark. This entity would assemble in one place elements of zoos, aquariums, botanic gardens, and natural history, anthropology, and other types of museums. (In our case we hope that the emphasis on holism would extend beyond the National Zoo to the Smithsonian itself. This would cross-reference, wherever possible, this huge and disparate institution. Airplanes in the National Air and Space Museum have obvious reference to flight in animals and plants—all are aerodynamics.) The biopark would make connections with the arts. Much of art, particularly aboriginal art, centers around nature, and the evolutionary design of many creatures is reflected in human creations. Convergence of function produces convergence of "design" in the living world and the world of human creativity. Attack and defense in the living world parallels in devices and processes the evolution of human warfare and weapons of offense and defense.

The first reaction to this concept is to suggest that this is just an extension of the "habitat zoo," which supposedly strives for realism in the creation of natural-looking habitat immersion exhibits. But here there is a fundamental misconception. What we humans call realism is a good reflection of our viewpoint, determined by our perceptual world. This inevitably gives rise to an anthropocentric distortion of biology. Most animals do not share our perceptual dominances. They may see more or less sharply, more or less to our scale (see the Pope quotation at the beginning of this chapter), in black and white, or in colors resembling or differing from our spectrum. They may be predominantly and acutely olfactory or microsmatic; have hearing better or worse than ours; have hearing that permits accurate echolocation or sonar; have electrical senses (as in fishes and some mammals); have an acute sense of taste or a poor one; and so on. We need exhibits that allow humans to appreciate the sensory worlds of other animals and how plants deal with external stimuli. The same applies with even more force to their behavioral imperatives of other organisms. All this is an extension beyond the anthropocentric habitat zoo. With all these elements of broad interconnectivity, the biopark thus becomes a vehicle for holism and a neo-encyclopedist philosophy.

The National Zoo has tried to break down the barriers of subject-exclusivity and interconnect with the broad stream of knowledge to the advantage of all. The expense of building holism, interactivity, and multiple sensory into new exhibits has not been excessive. In developing multisensory stimulation for visitors we have been deeply conscious of the attraction exerted by animal activity and the relatively non-stimulative effect of inactivity (sleeping, motionlessness) in our living collection. We have thus been attempting to achieve symmetry in stimulating activity in the visitors outside and the animals inside our exhibits. Exciting the imagination and stirring the affectional system are part of our ongoing programs.

Our cheetah exhibit, for instance, provides plenty of activity and interaction through a variety of means. It illustrates cheetah biology; the imperilment of the species; research on its present infertility; the cheetah in history; and the nature of predation. We highlight the cheetah's speed, its extraordinary stride, and its adaptations to being a short-burst "drag racer." For the animals we developed a pursuit device to stimulate them to typical bursts of high-speed chasing; this was both an exhibit device and a method of enriching the animals' lives and keeping them fit. We marked out on the zoo pathway the immense extent of a top-speed cheetah's stride and created a trail where children can stalk and run. The trail starts with a digital weighing scale referenced to lion, cheetah, and hyena prey. In the category of 150-200 pounds, visitors read that "Lions could kill something your size twice a week," or "A group of cheetahs could kill you, but don't worry about a single cheetah," or " A pack of hyenas . . . could finish you off in an hour." ("Spooky," as I overheard one kid say.) At the end of the trail is a cheetah wheel of fortune, which you spin to determine whether you catch your prey. The probabilities are based on field data. My favorite is "You catch a young gazelle, but while you are away a lion eats your cubs." Real life, not the peaceable kingdom!

There are reproductions of cheetah in art and an information cube about reproductive abnormalities in cheetah populations, providing plenty of action and interaction. The activities this exhibit makes possible—scanning, stalking, running, weighing, and spinning the wheel of fortune—provide a learning element absent from passive T.V. treatments of cheetah and impossible with video games. A video theater based on a large laserdisc player with a choice of seven programs adds an element that is impossible to provide by other means. It lets us present real scientists commenting on research into the complex problems confronting the cheetah populations in Africa, studies of reproductive enhancement by artificial insemination, in vitro fertilization, and embryo transplantation. This part of the exhibit has worked efficiently over all seasons and all kinds of weather and is attractive to visitors.

Every time I visit this exhibit with its marvelous animals I think of the electronic developments just around the corner. I think of a hand-held CD-ROM device that could be used as a portable multimedia supplement to this exhibit. It would replace our existing audio wands with their pacing problems, and give much more to the audience. A good portable CD-ROM player would allow the visitor, for instance, to watch a cheetah running and call up a video of its prey-capture behavior, its skeletal structure in cine X-ray, its internal organs, an audio of its heartbeat at rest and after exercise, and a view of the monochromatic perceptual world in which cats live. The visitor could finish up with a full-color print-out of the information that she had reviewed on tigers, cats in general, and the connecting links with the world of knowledge.

In the pollinarium, an exhibit on pollination attached to the zoo's invertebrate exhibit, we accomplish most of our goals effectively without complex electronics, using animals, plants, and models. The pollinarium, which opened in late 1995, illustrates the exquisite plant/animal synergy in the evolution of pollination adaptations. On display are butterflies of several species, hummingbirds, and three observation hives of honey bees arranged in an unconventionally massive semicircular complex. Visitors stand inside the semicircle, as though viewing the bees that have nested inside a tree. Three separate tubes connect these hives to the outside. Since this is an exhibit on plant/animal interactions the pollinarium is richly planted with flowers representing a broad spectrum of color, odor, and structure. Also included are plant species that are egg-laying sites and larval food plants for the butterflies. Together, the living components of the exhibit provide an expansively multimedia experience. Color, odor, movement, and sound combine with the tropical humidity and heat to assail the senses.

To interpret the activities for the visitor, we used a wide variety of models and interactive devices. These include a salvia (garden sage) flower large enough for children to emulate the pollinating bee by entering it. The complex, hinged anthers are activated by children who push against the lower parts, causing the top of the pollinator to swing down and dust the child's bottom with pollen. Above the flower is a very large model of the honey bee showing its pollen baskets, tongue, and hairs, which help it collect pollen and nectar from flowers. There are life-sized models of bats pollinating cactus, and rafflesia, the largest flower on Earth. There is also a large model of a pollen grain.

Graphic panels and simulated notebooks highlight various aspects of pollination biology. Visitors have the opportunity for direct investigation, watching bees in the three contiguous observation hives doing round- and waggle-dances. These are communicative behaviors that show the direction and distance of rich nectar resources. This very advanced bee "language" only needs a means of translation for visitors to identify the part of the zoo to which the dance points. Some kind of device could be attached to or near the glass wall of the hive on which the dancer's bearing could be matched. A simple 360-degree protractor with a moveable dial would work, provided that the sun's position could also be transferred to this plotter. Then a large-scale zoo map could provide a means of deciding where, in the real world, the nectar source was. This would be a unique form of interactive educational device—reading an animal's precise language in real time. Two years from writing this, I still I hope we can achieve it. Nowadays a simple piece of software might make this possible via a notebook computer located next to the hive, but simple mechanical devices are more robust.

One interactive display takes visitors beyond the human visible spectrum, at least by simulation. Most insects, and bees in particular, have a spectrum shifted to the ultra-violet end compared with our own. They have little or no red sensitivity but see a color called bee purple that is invisible to us. In the pollinarium, a display box contains a model flower that is shown in human-natural colors and, at the touch of a switch, as the bee would see it. Patterns invisible to us guide bees to many flowers. This is where a further multi-medium device could take us further, where we were limited by finances and logistics. It is possible to adapt a T.V. camera to "see" in the ultraviolet (Eisner et al. 1969, 1988). If we could make such a camera tamper proof, visitors could look at our wide range of flowers in real time and see a bee's eye view of their "hidden" markings. Perhaps we could just tape this and show it on a monitor. We deal with odor in another exhibit; perhaps we need another word to substitute for exhibit when the signal is smelled not seen.

The pollinarium is attached to the zoo's invertebrate exhibit, the first new exhibit to incorporate many of the biopark concepts. It deals with the more than 90 percent (probably more than 95 percent) of animal species that are not vertebrates. The exhibit was laid out with a simple path through the larger aquaria or animal holding areas that were designed to highlight the complexity, antiquity, economic and ecological importance, beauty, and wondrous nature of the many kinds of invertebrates. Art is displayed next to the animals, including Minoan stirrup cups and Amerindian images, along with Roman mosaics. In addition to these active and colorful displays—ranging from "protozoa" in a microtheater, to cuttlefish, octopus, and web-building spiders—there is a browsing area—an entirely interactive exploratorium of living animals. Here, visitors can explore objects under the microscope, watch crayfish with water glasses, test the responses of anemones to chemical stimulation, and identify insects with a special program on a touch-screen computer.

Computerized dichotomous keys have great advantages over the printed versions. The characters used for making determinations of genus and species frequently rely on comparisons of size, microstructures, color, and difficult-to-discern factors. The printed page does not readily present such options. The computer makes it much easier to guide the user through difficult comparisons. Our microtheater is a major advance in multimedia applications. It is also a simple step to take. Some of the most intriguing and beautiful animals are tiny creatures that live in water and are only visible through a microscope. To share this privileged view, we focus a high-sensitivity video camera down the microscope and connect it to a large-screen video monitor. The result is our visitors can see the glorious dance of the diatoms or the intricate movements of delightful marine plankton. The surface waters of our long-established coral tank are rich with organisms that I had never seen alive in my long career as a research biologist.

The Think Tank exhibit was designed to explore higher mental processes that can broadly be defined as "thinking" in non-human animals. This broad definition encompasses such subjects as language, counting, tool use, various kinds of learning, the manipulation of conspecific behaviors, and adaptive behavior. Brain size is also a prominent subject within this area. We have orangutans as the main living subjects, Celebes (now Sulawasi) macaques, leaf-cutter ants, and hermit crabs. The orangs live in the Great Ape House several hundred feet from the Think Tank building and commute to and fro on an overhead cableway called the O-Line. This innovative functional substitute for an arboreal pathway between the two buildings was a bold step based on careful study of the apes' abilities and known behavior. It has worked flawlessly, to our great satisfaction, and provides both a striking spectacle and an impressive learning experience for our visitors.

Thinking. Many of the exhibit's messages are best conveyed by objects, mechanical interactives, and animals. Others can only be communicated by video materials and computers. For instance, an introductory video shown on nine monitors positioned at various heights sets the scene for the entire exhibit. The video shows creatures, ranging from web-building spiders to wolves, carrying out complex activities, and in each case asks the question: Is this thinking? This is intentionally thought provoking. Does building something as complex as an orb-web involve thought? The answer is probably not. (As a student of spiders, I would say certainly not.) There is a definite advantage to using video at this point. There is no way that living spiders would build, or wolves hunt, repetitively at the entrance to the building. We can only do it this way. It is at once arresting and effective.

Brains and tools. Elsewhere, objects, models, and mechanical devices speak well. Bronze models of brains are all the better for being solid and touchable. An interactive mechanical device compares brain size to body size in a more direct and repeatable way than film.

The concept and definition of tools is central to the theme and is communicated by collections of human tools, ranging from prehistoric to modern, using both originals and replicas available for visual and tactile exploration in large boxes. Chimpanzee termite "fishing" tools are explored with a model termite mound. Hermit crabs, moving and watchable, are used to raise the question, "Is the shell a tool?" They don't grow it—they choose it and they carry it around. . . . It should be a tool—is it?

Best of all, in my view, are the tool-use experiments with the orangs themselves. Their Think Tank home has large windows facing a banked seating area for visitors. The windows have very large shelves on the visitor side and can open wide enough for the apes to put their hands and arms out. Zoo staff place solid and liquid food of various kinds out of reach on the shelf and give the orangs leafy branches as the raw materials for tool building. This has been the basis for simultaneous visitor education and research with the orangs. They have so far invented a honey-collecting tool and a juice-collecting tool that are the functional equivalent of spoons, and a rake for reaching and obtaining otherwise inaccessible pellet food. Much of this experimentation has been videotaped for subsequent use in the exhibit. It is extraordinarily fascinating and revelatory.

Language. The development of visitor thoughts on language is stimulated through a number of graphic panels and particularly through games. Syntax wheels allow visitors to study the effect of word placement in sentences and the function of "parts of speech." A tangram-derived puzzle is extended into an exercise in precise communication, by separating a visitor from a partner with a visual barrier. This forces the visitor to describe in words the pattern he is creating to his partner, the auditor/copyist. When all is complete the two compare the patterns they have constructed.

These and other ingenious tests and demonstrations set the scene for the *pièce de résistance*: The orangs are being taught an arbitrary symbolic language in which images represent numbers, nouns, adjectives, and verbs. Eventually, the symbols will be used in sentences. The keyboards used by the orang's teachers can be located outside the apes' living quarters. The apes' large monitor is a touchscreen model, allowing them to match displayed meanings to the symbols and eventually to talk back. What goes on in the process of symbol learning is visible on large monitors on the public side of the exhibit that mirror the screen on the orangs' side. This is an unusual use of electronic media in exhibits. We hope eventually to make it possible for the public to communicate with the apes, using a keyboard, monitor, and the zoo's orang language symbols. This dream is getting ever closer to reality.

The Shape of Things to Come

The prospect of portable, hand-held CD-ROM players has already arisen at the zoo, but a number of multimedia projects are already closer to completion. The Amazonia Gallery features working laboratories where the public is able to see, hear, etc., scientists and sense-expanding scientific equipment in action. A scanning electronic microscope reveals the ultra-small surface details of many animals and the details of ultra-small animals. A sound analysis machine used for studies of animal vocalizations can, time-permitting, produce sonographs on paper and on computer monitors. Our molecular biology unit has installed genetic analysis equipment in an office that permits public viewing. The gallery includes an Earth Situation Room where a giant globe rotates alongside a projector that produces large-scale computer-generated images of world climate patterns, seasonal shifts in the icecaps, ocean currents, and so on. We expect that this facility will eventually allow these images to be projected on the inside of the translucent globe instead of flat screens. As the software expands we will be able to address biogeography and climatic, traumatic, and anthropogenic perturbations of our planet.

Conclusion

The fundamental and probably atavistic attraction of living plants and animals will almost certainly survive any approaches to virtual reality that are made in this and the next century. If all our efforts to protect and conserve biodiversity are not in vain, sometime in the early part of the next millennium we may restore the glory of a predominantly intact and diverse biosphere. Even if this happens, unless our urbanized sprawl is limited by wise governments and the human population stabilizes at its present level, or better still is reduced peacefully, contact with real nature will not be improved. As a result, living bioexhibits will still be important for human educational, esthetic, cultural, and affective needs and pleasures. Such experiences of "natural" multimedia or multisensory reality will need to be coupled with whatever non-natural media interpretations enhance, extend, and interconnect knowledge. Projected holographic simulations with movement and virtual reality are not far away. One way to take ourselves into the perceptual worlds of other species, an urgent educational necessity, may be through this kind of future technology. One can imagine "seeing" the world with the sharpened olfactory perception, high-frequency audition, and monochromatic vision of a dog family species (perhaps the wolf ancestor of our domestic companions). What a mind-expanding experience this could be, both in terms of our rational and emotional nature. The holodeck may be built in museums and live bioexhibits before the possibilities for trekking the stars becomes real.

In the end all this will be possible only if the gloomy projections by the Roman historian Sallust 2,000 years ago and by Galbraith in this century are not fulfilled in the future. If resources are redirected to support our efforts we may yet expand intellectual horizons dramatically. On the other hand, if we somehow, against all present indications achieve an Edenesque Utopia, bioexhibits can gracefully wither away. It would be nice to think that sometime in the future we may not be needed.

References

American Association of Museums (AAM). 1992. *Excellence and equity: Education and the public dimension of museums*. Washington, D.C.: American Association of Museums.

_____. 1994. *Museums count*. Washington, D.C.: American Association of Museums.

Brzezinski, Z. 1993. *Out of control*. New York: MacMillan.

Dawkins, R. 1995. *River out of Eden. a Darwinian view of life*. New York: Basic Books.

Eisner, T., R. E. Silberglied, D. Aneshansley, J. E. Carrel, and H. C. Howland. 1969. Ultraviolet video-viewing: The television camera as an insect eye. *Science* 166: 1172-1174.

Eisner, T., D. Aneshansley, and M. Eisner. 1988. Ultraviolet viewing with a color television camera. *BioScience*. 38: 496-498.

Falk, J. H. and L. D. Dierking. 1992. *The museum experience*. Washington, D.C.: Whalesback Books.

Galbraith, J. K. 1963. *The affluent society*. Rev. ed. New York: NAL Dutton.

Hobsbawm, E. 1994. *The age of extremes*. New York: Pantheon.

Robinson, M. H. 1986. Zoos today and tomorrow. In *American Association of Zoological Parks and Aquariums 1986 regional proceedings*: 527-531.

_____. 1987a. Beyond the zoo: The biopark. *Defenders of Wildlife Magazine* 62(6):10-17

_____. 1987b. The actual and potential role of biological research in the development of exhibits. In *American Association of Zoological Parks and Aquariums' regional proceedings*: 12-18.

_____. 1987c. Towards the biopark: The zoo that is not. In *American Association of Zoological Parks and Aquariums 1987 annual conference proceedings*: 678-682.

_____. 1987d. Zoos today and tomorrow. *Place Magazine*, January/February 1987: 22-24.

_____. 1988a. Bioscience education through bioparks. *Bioscience* 38:630-634.

_____. 1988b. Zoos today and tomorrow. *People, Animals, Environment* 6, no. 1 (Spring 1988): 29-32.

_____. 1989a. Overture to a new zoo: The National Zoo's invertebrate house. *Freshwater and Marine Aquarium* 12:104-134.

_____. 1989b. Homage to Niko Tinbergen and Konrad Lorenz: Is classical ethology relevant to zoos? *Zoo Biology* 8:1-13.

_____. 1989c. The zoo that is not. *Conservation Biology* 3: 213-215.

_____. 1991a. Animal rights, objections to zoos, and the evolution of bioparks. *International Union of Directors of Zoological Gardens, conference 1990, Singapore, scientific proceedings*: 18-45.

_____. 1991b. Invertebrates: exhibiting the silent majority. *International Zoo Yearbook* 30: 1-7.

_____. 1992. Global change, the future of biodiversity, and the future of zoos. *Biotropica* 24: 345-352.

_____. 1993a. Biodiversity, bioparks, and saving ecosytems. *Endangered Species Update* 10: 52-57.

_____. 1993b. The age of the biopark. *The World & I* (September 1993): 228-233.

_____. 1994. The new zoo and the old adam. *Museum News* 73, no. 1: 30-43.

Pope, A. 1733. (1994.) *An essay on man.* New York: Dover Publications.

Wilson, E. O. 1986. *Biophilia.* Cambridge, Mass.: Harvard University Press.

chapter 4

Audience and Accessibility
Lynn D. Dierking and John H. Falk

What are visitors' expectations for a museum visit? Museum audiences—whether families, adult couples, or singles—agree on a few characteristics: 1) the best museum presents a variety of interesting material that appeals to different age groups, educational levels, personal interests, and technical levels; 2) visitors expect to be mentally, and perhaps physically, engaged by what they see, experiencing a personal connection with the objects, ideas, and experiences presented; and 3) people visiting in groups, both families with children and adult groups, expect a shared experience, allowing everyone to exchange and communicate their knowledge and excitement about what they see and experience. Of course, there are also some built-in assumptions. Paramount is the knowledge that this is the real stuff or about the real stuff; consequently, visitors believe that there is an inherent sense of integrity to the objects, ideas, and experiences presented within the museum (Falk and Dierking 1992; Shoup and Associates 1995).

Referring to what makes a museum visit engaging, some visitors mention "hands-on" or "touching" experiences; others indicate a desire for a human presence in the galleries to respond to specific visitor questions and to provide explanations; and many refer to the role that media can play in fostering interactivity, particularly CD-

Lynn D. Dierking is associate director, and John Falk is director, Institute for Learning Innovation (formerly Science Learning, inc.), Annapolis, Md., a non-profit research and development organization that helps museums and other community-based organizations better serve their publics.

ROMs and computer interactives. A universal theme emerges from these descriptions: all reflect a reciprocal relationship in which the visitor is given choices, makes choices, becomes involved, and ultimately is an active participant in the experience. This is true whether the visitor becomes curious and asks a question of a staff member on the gallery floor, experiences something new by encountering or touching an object for the first time or in a different way, or simply chooses among options on a computer terminal.

It has been our belief for many years that in terms of their responsibility to the public, museums are primarily free-choice learning environments; we have been known to refer to them as public institutions for personal learning (Falk and Dierking 1995). Media is an important and powerful means for museums to present learning options to their visitors, in the same way that a well-trained docent or well-designed hands-on exhibit offers different but equally valid choices. Media, well designed and wisely used, can play an important role in ensuring that these environments inspire and provoke curiosity and further understanding among visitors with varying backgrounds, interests, and knowledge levels.

This chapter will explore why media represents an important presentation option for museums in terms of both audience and conceptual accessibility. Because our opinions have been formed in part by our many years of audience research, we also will share some of our work that has focused on media use by museum visitors, answering such questions as: Who uses media in museums? Are media users different from non-media users? From visitors' perspectives, what are some of the pros and cons of media use in museums? And finally, as the museum field further embraces media as a presentation option, we will raise important questions that we believe the field should be asking regarding the relationships among object, venue, and visitor, exploring how media can best be used to enhance the visitor experience within the museum.

Media as a Presentation Option in Museums

Media can provide a variety of learning options to visitors, in part because newer technologies can provide choices in terms of what is experienced and, in many cases, how it is experienced. Many visitors—even those who are not sophisticated users of technology—recognize that computers, CD-ROMs, and other technologies can provide both varying degrees of depth of information and options that improve visitor flexibility and choice (Shoup and Associates 1995). Why is this so important? Learning is a highly personal, idiosyncratic process. People have preferred modes of perceiving and processing information; memory storage and retrieval are also highly idiosyncratic processes shaped to a large degree by a person's previous experience, knowledge, feelings, and physical well-being (Falk and Dierking, forthcoming). What this suggests for those of us in the business of designing learning experiences for visitors is that we should be seeking techniques that maximize choice. Media provides one such viable option.

Media is already, and will continue to be, critical for interactivity, especially for today's children who are comfortable with technology, and find it easy to use. For better or for worse, particularly when considering engaging children and young adults, many adult visitors feel that museums must utilize media as a presentation option: "Because kids have so many alternatives, the museums have to engage them in the ways they need." Media-rich exhibitions can create museum-comfort today for tomorrow's museum-going public.

Media also has the power to attract potential new audiences or to present new dimensions to visitors. While working on a summative evaluation of computer interactives focused on connoisseurship at the Winterthur Museum, for example, we encountered a male visitor who "had been dragged" to the museum by his wife. In his 50s, this fellow had tried over the years to appreciate Winterthur, one of his wife's favorite museums, but up until this visit had not successfully accomplished this goal. While visiting this time, however, he happened upon the connoisseurship interactives and spent the rest of his visit (almost an hour) interacting with the computer programs. (Most visitors spend about 15 minutes in the exhibition.) As a university math educator very interested in the use of computers for teaching algebra, he was fascinated by the design of the program and some of the information it contained. He indicated that the programs had given him a whole new appreciation for the Winterthur collection that many previous visits to the institution had not afforded. In that same study, another male visitor in his 50s, who was very interested in decorative arts and Winterthur, said the programs engaged him and allowed him to learn some things he had not known previously. A number of female visitors also indicated high interest and enjoyment in the interactives. In fact, evaluators observed no gender differences in use at all (Dierking and Marcum 1994; Dierking and Harper 1995).

We are not suggesting that media should be the only mode of presentation utilized in a museum. The focal point of the experience should always be the object, phenomena, and/or ideas that are a part of the institution's mission. Well-designed and well-used media can be an important tool in the museum's storytelling repertoire, but it represents only one communication strategy.

Media and the Interpretation of Ideas

Media also plays an important role in interpreting certain specific ideas, helping to make them more accessible to more visitors. As we have suggested, museums focus on the objects and phenomena that they collect and present; by their very nature these tend to be concrete and/or observable. However, rarely are the ideas they embody equally concrete and observable. Increasingly, the messages are abstract and complex, requiring tremendous leaps for many visitors who may not have the depth of understanding or knowledge to easily follow the story line. Exacerbating this situation is the fact that objects and discrete phenomena often are not the best medium to convey complex abstractions (Falk, Koran, and Dierking 1986; Falk and Dierking 1992). Media, on the other hand, with its power to juxtapose and visually and aurally connect ideas, is an excellent vehicle for presenting abstractions. Because of its inherently powerful visual and aural characteristics, media can support and complement presentation and interpretation in ways that the objects and phenomena alone may not be able to do.

For example, during a summative evaluation study of the National Museum of American History's "American Encounters" exhibit, visitors who watched even a portion of the three films in the exhibition were much better at articulating the big conceptual ideas of the exhibition than visitors who merely looked at objects and read labels. This ability persisted over several months. In this particular

case, the combination of film, objects, and labels was a more powerful and effective medium for conveying the abstract ideas of cultural
conflict and cross-cultural events in New Mexico than were objects
and labels alone (Falk and Holland 1994). The introductory film to
"Seeds of Change" at the National Museum of Natural History served
a similar role for visitors to that exhibition.

In addition to broad, over-arching concepts, media has the
capacity to illustrate change and dynamism, attributes difficult to
convey in typical static displays. Two examples of this use of media
come from the National Museum of Natural History. In "Life in the
Ancient Seas," a "claymation" film loop showed the effects of changing temperatures on ocean life populations, while in the new Geology, Gems, and Minerals Hall, stories related to process concepts such
as plate tectonics, mountain formation, and the dynamic rock cycle
are presented by animation and a computer interactive. The museum could have communicated these concepts through words in a
label, but presenting them visually through media represented a better communication choice in these situations.

Media also can place objects in their appropriate historical
and/or cultural context. This helps visitors to better understand
objects and to transcend their concrete characteristics. We have
observed this in a few cases where media presentations were used
effectively as orientation devices. For example, a media program
serves as an effective orientation for a single exhibition: "18th Century Life" at the National Museum of American History. The appro-
priately short and focused program presents the processes of history
and how historians understand it, giving visitors a totally different
perspective than they might normally take in such an object-rich
exhibition. We also have seen media used effectively to orient visitors to an entire museum experience. The Cahokia Mound Visitor
Center just outside St. Louis, Mo., is one such site. A film introducing
the visitor to life in an early Cahokia village ends to reveal the noise,
movement, and activity of the community. As a scrim is raised up,
one realizes that the theater is actually in the middle of a simulated
village, which is itself in the middle of the visitor center. The activity
and silhouettes creating the program's eerie, life-like quality are actually other visitors walking through the village portion of the exhibition, and the noises include visitors' voices and pre-recorded sounds

such as dogs barking and stone tools being used. This powerful orientation experience continues throughout the visit since the visitor center's exhibitions are on the perimeter of the village, where one can still hear the dogs and the tools. This provides a wonderfully rich context for the objects and artifacts.

Finally, for some museums, media increasingly is the object. In the U.S. Holocaust Memorial Museum's temporary exhibition, "Liberation, 1945," some of the most powerful "objects" were the film footage shot as the concentration camps were liberated. Although some of this footage was edited before being placed as video loops in the exhibition, these film archives represent an invaluable part of the exhibition and museum's collection. The history of the 20th century is recorded on film. In the information age we will probably expect more of our collections to be composed of media than ever before.

Media and Visitors

What does audience research reveal about the use of media in exhibitions? One major generalization is that media use is highly self-selected. In several studies, not all visitors interacted with all of the media elements in any exhibition, just as few visitors read all the labels or look at all of the objects in an exhibition. For example, during the aforementioned Winterthur study, in which so many visitors were enthusiastic about the computer interactives, there were also people who expressed no interest at all in using the interactives or only used them minimally. Some typical responses by this group were: "I would rather spend my time looking at the objects themselves" and "I work with computers all week and so when I come to a museum I don't choose to do so."

Similar results were observed at several science centers during studies of the computer interactives in the traveling exhibition "What About AIDS?" (Falk and Holland 1992; Falk and Holland 1993; Holland and Falk 1995), of a film and videodisc in the "Spirit of the Motherland" exhibition at the Virginia Museum of Fine Arts (Dierking and Spencer-Etienne 1995; Dierking, Adams, and Spencer-Etienne 1996), of films in the "American Encounters" exhibition at the National Museum of American History (Falk and Holland 1994), and of films and video loops in the "Liberation, 1945" exhibition at the U.S. Holocaust Memorial Museum (Dierking, Falk, and Abrams, forthcoming). These are very different institutions, but we saw very similar results. It is important to note, of course, that in each of these studies there were a number of visitors that spent a great deal of quality time interacting with the media elements. These results support the notion that media is an important option for *some* visitors.

Beyond the quality of the presentations or visitor interest in the material presented, a number of factors can influence media use by museum audiences. One important factor is the physical context in which the media presentation takes place. Visitors are more likely to watch films if seating of some kind is provided and if they feel like they can spend some time without impeding other people's experience. If the film or video loop is in a busy corridor with no space set aside where people can sit comfortably, visitors will be less likely to view presentations in their entirety.

Social factors can also affect visitor use of media. Computer work stations that seem to afford access by only a single individual can discourage use by family or all-adult groups—even those interested in computers. Since the vast majority of people visit museums with friends or family, computer interactives should be designed to accommodate groups. The spaces should invite group participation. For example, there should be more than one chair and large screens so that more than one individual can see. These simple strategies can permit social groups to use media together.

Visitors' time budgets or perceived time budgets also influence their use of media. Very few people enter the museum without some concept of how much time they will spend; most spend one to two hours. Consequently, the majority of visitors won't watch long films or videodiscs; 15 to 20 minutes for any individual exhibition component, regardless of quality, is a huge investment if one is only spending an hour in the whole museum. This does not mean that there are not visitors willing to make a large time commitment; if they are interested in the material being presented or fascinated by the technology, they will spend the time. But museums can increase the likelihood that more visitors will at least get some of the points of a presentation by providing levels of information. With a small time investment, all visitors should be able to get the main points; others interested in more in-depth material can spend more time. It is also important for museums to better inform visitors about what these options are; perception is as important as reality. If visitors *feel* that the time investment will be too great, they may decide to skip a film or computer interactive.

Who Uses Media in Museums?

Can one make any generalizations about who uses media in museums? Here it is important to make some distinctions about the type of media being discussed. Films, video loops, and animations that are integrated into exhibitions (as opposed to stand-alone IMAX films or introductory films that often channel all visitors into viewing them) tend to be used in varying amounts by visitors, generally depending on how long they have been in the museum or particular exhibition, or how interested they are in the information presented. Visitors who encounter these media elements early in their visit or who are very interested in the topic may be extremely attentive. They will attempt to watch a number of media presentations as thoroughly as possible until museum fatigue and the press of time make them more selective. Once in this "selective" mode, visitors will scan the screen briefly or watch the film for a few seconds. Only if this brief "sound bite" provokes their interest will they stay to watch the remainder.

On the other hand, much more self-selection seems to operate among visitors when computer interactives and videodiscs offer choices. Perhaps it is the technical knowledge or the perception thereof needed to operate them, or just a personal preference for acquiring information in this way, but such media seems to be less universally used by all visitors, and is used intensively by only a subset of visitors. As discussed earlier, children and youth are drawn to such media, as are people with some knowledge of computers or other advanced technologies. But there are still a number of people, particularly visitors 50 years and older, who are intimidated by computers and videodiscs. These individuals often believe that some special knowledge or skill is required to successfully interact with the machine. Two women in their 50s observed during the Winterthur study were confused by a touch screen and kept looking for the buttons. "Where are the buttons?" they wondered out loud. (It is important to note that there were a number of technological novices in this study who persisted in their efforts to use the computer interactives; despite some initial setbacks, they were highly successful and pleased with the experience.) As with exhibit designers, computer interactive and videodisc designers still sometimes assume too much about visitors' technical knowledge and their ability to comprehend subtle directions or graphic elements. Although the public is becoming increasingly computer-savvy, it is important not to assume too much about what visitors know about computers and other media options.

Are media users different from non-media users? As suggested, media users tend to be younger visitors and those visitors who feel comfortable with the technology. This is especially true when one is considering visitor use of such media as computer interactives and videodiscs. Gender is also an interesting factor when considering media use. Only a limited number of studies have investigated the relationship between media use and gender in the museum setting. In one study, more males were direct users of the computer, but both genders were equally represented as indirect users (Pawlukiewicz, Bohling, and Doering 1989). In another study of touch-screen computers as an orientation device, 65 percent of the users were males (Sharpe 1983). In a 1991 study by Morrissey of an interactive videodisc in an exhibit on birds, groups with boys were twice as likely to use the program as groups with girls, although the results were more equivocal when adults were in the group (Morrissey 1991). In our recent formative evaluation of a computer interactive for the "How Things Fly" gallery at the National Air and Space Museum (Abrams and Dierking 1996), 71 percent of the self-selected sample were males, while in a recent summative evaluation of an interactive videodisc in the "Spirit of the Motherland" exhibition at the Virginia Museum of Fine Arts, users were more prevalently female (Dierking, Adams, and Spencer-Etienne 1996). Gender is not as straightforward a variable as once considered.

We recently completed a remedial evaluation of the National Gallery of Art's Micro Gallery, an area on the first floor of the West Wing that provides videodisc access and in-depth information about the museum's collection (Adams, Abrams, and Falk 1996). Part of this study involved trying to determine how many people use the Micro Gallery and whether they were representative of the

National Gallery's usual visitors. Results suggested that there was a great deal of self-selection going on at the entrance of the gallery in terms of who goes in and who does not. For the most part, visitors to the Micro Gallery were representative of other gallery visitors. The main difference related to their level of ease with technology or their interest in getting more information about the National Gallery's collection from a videodisc. Among more than 100 visitors whom we observed and interviewed, only a few had come to the museum that day expressly to visit the Micro Gallery. The vast majority of Micro Gallery users were not aware of it prior to entering the museum.

This study, as well as the Virginia Museum of Fine Arts and Winterthur studies, also provide data that reduce, if not eliminate, a major concern that many skeptical museum professionals have about the use of media by visitors in exhibitions. There is no evidence that visitors choose to use a media element rather than look at objects and read labels in an exhibition. In fact, there is some modest evidence suggesting that some of these media presentations, such as the Micro Gallery, the *Spirit of the Motherland* videodisc and the *Experience Africa* film at the Virginia Museum of Fine Arts, and the connoisseurship interactives at Winterthur, actually serve as resources and incentives for visitors to look at objects again or in more depth. The media presentation alone is not the museum experience for visitors; they come expecting to look at and examine objects and/or phenomena and they do so. The media presentation is one aspect of the experience, but in no way the whole experience.

Visitor Attitudes Towards Media

In the minds of visitors, what are some of the pros and cons of media use in museums? Obviously, visitors are interested in the fact that media—particularly computers and videodiscs—can increase their options and choices. They recognize that in many cases technology helps museums, especially institutions wishing to serve children and youth, become more interactive. They recognize that computers and CD-ROM technology can provide choices in terms of the depth of information presented, as well as what is presented and, in many cases, how it is presented.

However, visitors have concerns about technology too. High

on visitors' list of complaints are media malfunctions and break-downs. As summarized by one Cleveland woman: "Nothing is more frustrating than going in and finding something that doesn't work. Very frustrating!" Visitors realize that new technology becomes dated quickly: "Today everything is high-tech and changes so much, tomorrow it's old-hat." "Things do get old, greater change makes it more interesting for kids and adults." "Make something more than a one-time experience, but a continually enriching one."

Access to museum media is a problem, too. Adult visitors frequently express concerns about their ability to access media, par-ticularly computer interactives and videodiscs, when there are large numbers of children or youth in the museum. This is only partially due to overcrowding; often it is caused by intimidation: "Technology is good for kids, but challenges some adults, and seeing kids clus-tered around terminals is intimidating to some adults." "Kids line up to push a button, so it's better to have more than one."

Visitors would like museums to be more "user-friendly," helping them understand what options are available. Once they make their choice, visitors want a successful experience. Visitors often suggest integrating "quick message" stations into exhibits to provide an overview function. These visitors would then put addi-tional terminals, reserved as "study stations," in dedicated areas or rooms where those interested can delve into the subject in more depth without tying up the limited number of machines placed in the heart of the exhibition.

Of course, in many ways much of this debate is moot. While media is but one option for interactivity (and we agree with Selma Thomas's comment that it is not media that brings people to the museum), visitors—particularly to science museums and science centers—increasingly expect to encounter some type of media expe-rience at a museum. This could be an IMAX film, a computer inter-active, or a videodisc—the particular media is not the issue. As Thomas argues, the museum field has brought this upon itself by feeling the need to update its techniques to attract new visitors. How-ever, these expectations would be there anyway. Media is ever-pre-sent in our society, and it would be foolish for museum exhibits not to wisely embrace such technologies, as have other museum depart-ments, such as collections and marketing. In our opinion, the issue for the field is not whether museums should utilize media, but how best to use it to enhance audience and conceptual accessibility. Having said this, what are some important issues and questions facing the museum field as media and high-technology presentation modes are increasingly utilized?

Questions for the Future

First and foremost, museums should seriously consider whether to use a media presentation at all; once that decision is made, they must select the most appropriate form. Decisions should be based on conceptual, aesthetic, intellectual, and technical considerations. All too often, decisions are based on budgetary concerns or made in response to the notion that every exhibit *must* have a media component. Each decision should be made independently, attempting to determine which presentation style will best highlight the objects and/or phenomena and best interpret related messages for the public.

We must ensure that poor use of media does not jeopardize the integrity and quality of what is presented in a museum. Museums don't automatically resort to superficial entertainment when they use media, as some in the profession believe. To avoid perpetuating this stereotype, however, we must maintain high standards of conceptual, aesthetic, intellectual, and technical standards at all times. Visitors assume that there is an inherent integrity to the objects, ideas, and experiences presented within the museum, and we have an obligation to uphold their trust.

This integrity includes communication. A museum can create the most wonderful media experience in the world, but if visitors do not know it is available or do not understand how to use it effectively, all that effort has been wasted. Whenever possible, formative testing of interfaces should be conducted with visitors during the development of computer interactives and videodiscs. This testing can be modest and can utilize paper mock-ups; it helps determine whether directions and touch-screen graphics communicate their purpose clearly to visitors. Storyboards and proposed screens for computer interactives should also be tested. As with exhibitions, small changes in presentation can result in large changes in comprehension. Finally, the location of these experiences within the exhibition also requires careful thought and planning and can significantly benefit from formative testing.

The museum field must get better at understanding the role that media plays in interpreting objects and ideas for people. Much audience research takes the form of focused evaluation studies, investigating the use of media in very specific situations, such as assessing the effectiveness of particular screens or directions in a computer interactive. Very little research has concentrated on larger topics such as who is drawn to media or the role that media can play in communicating complex, abstract ideas. Studies of this nature would yield significantly better media decisions. Other potentially interesting questions might be: What types of ideas lend themselves to particular types of media presentations? Is there a visitor profile for a "typical" media user? What types of orientation experiences support visitor learning? What role does authenticity play in the visitor experience in museums? How do media presentations facilitate/hinder perceptions of authenticity in the museum? As we begin to develop a better body of knowledge about the interpretive roles media can play, we will be in a much better position to wisely use media to support positive visitor experiences within museums.

References

Abrams, C. and L. D. Dierking. 1996. Evaluation results for four interactive prototypes: "How Things Fly" gallery development, interim report #3. Annapolis, Md.: Science Learning, inc.

Adams, M., C. Abrams, and J. Falk. 1996. Evaluation report: Micro Gallery, National Gallery of Art. Annapolis, Md.: Science Learning, inc.

Dierking, L. D. and D. V. R. Harper. 1995. Developing and evaluating computer interactives in a decorative arts museum." In *Current Trends in Audience Research and Evaluation* 9. Washington, D.C.: American Association of Museums' Committee on Audience Research and Evaluation.

Dierking, L. D. and U. Marcum. 1994. Winterthur Museum computer interactives summative evaluation. Annapolis, Md.: Science Learning, inc.

Dierking, L. D. and M. Spencer-Etienne. 1995. Summative report: Spirit of the Motherland Experience Africa video theater, Virginia Museum of Fine Arts. Annapolis, Md.: Science Learning, inc.

Dierking, L. D., M. Adams, and M. Spencer-Etienne. 1996. Evaluation report: Interactive videodisc, Virginia Museum of Fine Arts. Annapolis, Md.: Science Learning, inc.

Dierking, L. D., J. H. Falk, and C. Abrams. Forthcoming. Summative evaluation of "Liberation, 1945," U.S. Holocaust Memorial Museum. Annapolis, Md.: Science Learning, inc.

Falk, J. H. and L. D. Dierking. 1992. *The museum experience.* Washington, D.C.: Whalesback Books.

———. Forthcoming. *How people learn when they don't have to.* Washington, D.C.: Whalesback Books.

Falk, J. H. and D. Holland. 1992. Formative evaluation of the AIDS traveling exhibition, "What about AIDS?," New York Hall of Science. Annapolis, Md.: Science Learning, inc.

———. 1993. Remedial evaluation results: "What about AIDS?" traveling exhibition. Annapolis, Md.: Science Learning, inc.

———. 1994. Summative evaluation: Visitors' use of "American Encounters." Annapolis, Md.: Science Learning, inc.

Falk, J. H., J. J. Koran, Jr., and L. D. Dierking. 1986. The things of science: Assessing the learning potential of science museums. *Science Education* 70, no. 5: 503-508.

Holland, D. and J. H. Falk. 1995. Continuing summative evaluation results: "What about AIDS?" traveling exhibition. Annapolis, Md.: Science Learning, inc.

Morrissey, K. 1991. Visitor behavior and interactive video. *Curator* 34, no. 2: 109-118.

Pawlukiewicz, J., K. Bohling, and Z. Doering. 1989. The Caribou connection: Will people stop, look and question? Paper presented at the American Association of Museums, May 15, 1989, Washington, D.C.

Sharpe, E. 1983. *Touch screen computers: An experimental orientation device at the National Museum of American History.* Washington, D.C.: National Museum of American History, Smithsonian Institution.

Shoup and Associates. 1995. Focus group investigation: Evaluation of the Reinberger Hall of Earth and Planetary Exploration. Cleveland, Ohio: Cleveland Museum of Natural History.

chapter 5

Media, Art Museums, and Distant Audiences

Ruth R. Perlin

Recently, a group of fourth- and fifth-graders were on a tour of the sculpture of Claes Oldenburg at the National Gallery of Art in Washington, D.C. They stopped at a prominently featured work, and the docent asked if the children recognized the object represented. The children offered no suggestions and, in fact, were silent. Finally, the docent said that the large form represented a typewriter eraser. One of the children then asked, "What is a typewriter?"!

Aside from the questions this raises about the "decontextualizing" of art in the museum setting, the incident is revealing in a more general sense: When this child was born, typewriters (and typewriter erasers) could be found in most offices and schools. But in the few years since his birth, the world has changed enormously and, along with it, frames of reference for both individuals and institutions. Oldenburg is surely aware of this, as his works not only raise issues about the nature of common objects and our perceptions of them but also address issues of obsolescence. In confronting his works, we are challenged to question our collective, modern faith in machines and emerging technologies. Clearly, issues of new and altered realities have extensive implications for the arts, for art museums, and for our audiences.

Ruth R. Perlin is head, Department of Education Resources, Education Division, National Gallery of Art, Washington, D.C. She has produced a variety of nationally distributed educational programs, including six award-winning films on American artists.

Technology

What do we mean when we speak of "technology" or "the new technologies?" In general parlance, we mean the merging of a number of communications media—sound, text, and visual elements (still and moving images, photography)—into a composite medium generally referred to as multimedia. In the multimedia environment, the three primary modes of communication—words, images, sound—are integrated. Their confluence and the ease with which we can move among them and translate one form to another offer opportunities for interactivity among elements as well as between the media and the individual. Encompassing all of these media in the computer context allows both content providers (or producers) and users to link and combine information—including images—in whatever way they choose, offering multiple pathways through a body of content.

Access and Distant Audiences

At one of the first conferences devoted to museums and education, the late Frank Oppenheimer, who "invented," founded, and directed the Exploratorium in San Francisco, spoke about the educational role of museums. He said that the "thing that both art and science have in common . . . or one of the things . . . is that they are both increasingly concerned with the inaccessible . . . " (Larrabee 1968, p. 214).

He was, of course, referring to both meaning and access. As an art museum educator, I share with my colleagues that task of trying to make the inaccessible accessible and significant. The crux of museum education is the accessibility, in the broadest sense, of our collections and exhibitions to the public. Most museums view educating and informing audiences as a matter of importance. A corollary of this belief is the concept that education is contingent on the public's access to museum resources; namely, our collections and the range of accompanying information. The interpretative or educative role means considerably more, though, than a simple "open-door policy." Much thought and energy are devoted to developing ways in which objects and collections can be more effectively understood. Programs for interpretation—guided or recorded tours, lectures, symposia, films, and other multimedia presentations—are all carried out for the benefit of museum visitors.

However, by focusing only on programs that take place within the museum setting, we overlook those people who cannot visit the museum and those works of art that may not be on view. To address this situation, the National Gallery of Art has long supported programs for national audiences—a challenging educational responsibility—which are somewhat different from the traditional museum programs that focus primarily on nearby audiences and museum visitors.

I have spent much of my professional career as an art historian/museum educator engaged in developing, producing, and disseminating educational resources for use by educational and cultural organizations across the country, chiefly in the nation's schools. One of my primary concerns has been to provide resources that meet the needs of such a vast, diverse, and distant audience and reflect the multiplicity and variety of the nation's population and its educational constituencies. Across the country there are enormous differences in students and in teachers, in settings ranging from elementary schools to universities to continuing education programs, and countless demographic and geographic variations, from small villages and towns to large metropolitan areas. The educational system in the United States is itself extremely varied, with individual states establishing curricula—the content and sequence of subjects studied—and authorizing instructional resources. And there are county-by-county variations on these centrally mandated requirements. An additional factor concerns the kind of media used in schools. Often the computers in classrooms are out-of-date, lacking screens capable of showing a full range of color, or the capacities, speed, and memory needed for refined and responsive presentation of images. And images are of paramount importance to those of us in art museums. Clearly, this situation may not pertain in years to come; nevertheless, we must acknowledge the existence of obsolete or antiquated equipment, hardware, and software in school settings. And even now we cannot assume the presense in the classroom of image-capable, functional work stations, with or without Internet connections. Moreover, there seems to be some doubt as to the extent to which our older, but densely populated, urban schools can be fitted with the cabling needed for electronic networking.

In view of this, what are some of the considerations that affect the development of both the content and the form of programs intended for use beyond the museum's walls? Given the extremely heterogeneous character of distant audiences, museums must provide resources that are adaptable to the innumerable special needs of varied groups at diverse sites across the nation and around the world. Not every program form will be useful to every segment of the audience. One must provide a variety—print-based slide programs, audiocassettes, teaching packets, as well as films or videocassettes and new media forms—and monitor the use of new technologies in order to offer audiences up-to-date options. Of equal importance is the range of topics of programs offered. For example, programs might include monographic treatments of artists or explorations of a period, styles, or national schools, and so on. Modular in design, program components are an assemblage, a collective resource from which audiences can select appropriate images and information and reconfigure them to suit individual needs and interests. The programs, taken together, are collections of resources, as are the elements within the programs themselves. Choice among programs and program elements permits individuals great latitude in adapting materials to their needs and allows learner and teacher to select those parts of the programs that are most relevant to their educational objectives. This flexibility of use is one of the underlying principles of program design and leads conceptually to recognizing and using the unique capabilities of new technologies.

In 1979, I directed a project to develop a videodisc, a medium that was new to museums and in which I had long been interested. At that time, the videodisc answered our need for a higher degree of flexibility in program content, design, and use, and reflected our interest in offering our audiences newer types of programs. Videodisc technology addressed our commitment to providing and enhancing access to the National Gallery's resources, and thus was entirely consistent with our educational mission. The videodisc contained video programs about the institution and the art within the collections. But its most significant aspect was a still-frame "catalogue" of works in all media, a modest base from which a variety of programs and applications might be developed. We saw the videodisc as a visual compendium from which individuals could design programs to meet their own objectives rather than offering an embedded program.

Our most recent videodisc, *American Art from the National Gallery of Art*, produced in 1993, contains a brief video segment that provides an overview of American art, but its largest and most significant component is a still-frame catalogue. With more than 2,600 works of art and three times that number of close-up details, it constitutes a comprehensive survey of American painting, sculpture, and works on paper from the National Gallery's collections. Although the current publication and presentation medium is in videodisc form, we created an extensive digital image base as the source for every image and detail. Using digital imaging represented a quantum leap for us, for the digital environment permits the most desirable attributes of program content and presentation to be brought together in an eminently flexible and responsive form.

Digital Images

In regard to images—their capture and configuration, their appearance and presentation—the electronic environment can be dazzling in its options, exquisitely refined, and excruciatingly demanding. However, the digital resources we have created and are continuing to develop have a value of their own, far beyond that of a specific project or program. Digital images do not degenerate like slides and photographs and, therefore, one can create an "exemplar image" as the standard by and from which all other replicas are derived. All digital images are, in effect, "originals." They can be altered or modified without risk to the original work of art—both a benefit and a disadvantage of the medium. Equally important, images captured digitally can be stored on hard drives, CD-ROMs, videodiscs, diskettes, magnetic or optical discs, or other storage media. They can be retrieved quickly to serve a range of needs, from scholarly to entertainment. And they can be used again and again as the source for programs in almost any form, including printed materials. For example, we use the large group of digital images produced for the American art project and for a current project encompassing the rest of our collections as the image base for our collections management system data

Figure 1: Charles A. Brown & Co. Cheap Bookstore, Philadelphia (detail), c. 1854. Courtesy of The Library Company of Philadelphia. From the film Important Information Inside: John F. Peto and the Idea of Still-Life Painting, *Department of Extension Programs, National Gallery of Art, Washington, D.C., 1984.*

Figure 2: John F. Peto, Job Lot Cheap *(1892). The Fine Arts Museums of San Francisco; gift of Mr. and Mrs. John D. Rockefeller 3rd, 1979.7.81.*

and the museum's Web site. Digital images also are used by museum staff in a variety of internal institutional activities as well as for programs for the public—visitors to our buildings and those audiences well beyond the physical and geographic limits of the museum.

Context and a Broader Reality

One of the key interpretative aspects of media, or multimedia, is that it provides access to a broader reality—the larger world, past and present. When dealing with both distant audiences and those within the museum, we have found that offering glimpses of "the artist's reality" helps to enhance the audience's understanding and connections to works of art. For example, in a series of films on American artists, we traveled to the location where each artist lived, and tried to capture the environment and show its relationship to the art. A bridge between the artist's time and our own, whether achieved by archival images or live footage, enhances the audience's sense of the artist's life and work, and provides people with a richer context because of its greater authenticity.

An example is a film we produced on the late 19th-century still-life painter, John F. Peto. In that program we used archival photographs and live footage extensively. One of the photographs (figure 1) depicts a 19th-century view from the building in Philadelphia where Peto had his studio. The scene in the photograph corresponds with astonishingly similar elements in the artist's paintings (figure 2). Other paintings by Peto show his own objects, still on display today in the Island Heights, N.J., house and studio he built around 1890. Such visual and physical relationships illuminate an artist's merging of life and art.

Other Considerations in Programs for Distant Audiences

When one produces programs for distant audiences, achieving a sense of directness and immediacy is essential. For instance, in audiocassettes that accompany slide programs, our curators' comments on works of art are not scripted in advance but are structured carefully before a recording is made. Judicious editing creates the

impression that the curator is speaking conversationally and sponta-
neously to the listener. The same procedure is used by many museums for audio guides to exhibitions, which are also frequently
enhanced by music and other sounds related to the subject. This is
not entirely "natural." One has to employ a degree of artifice to create a sense of the real, the immediate, and the authentic, and that is
an important element of programs that are intended for distant audiences. We not only have to overcome physical, geographical distances but psychological, social, and educational ones as well.

The newer media provides an experience of directness and
immediacy by enabling the user to become an active participant in
the program, controlling what is seen and moving among ideas and
images at will. Art museums are among the institutions that have
been most beguiled by the promise of new technologies. They
embraced multimedia early on for the same reasons they looked to
more traditional media: to introduce and illuminate the visual arts.
But it should be recognized that media and the new technologies are
not ends in themselves; they represent powerful *means* for educating
the public and integrating art into their lives. Media programs—films,
video, and videodiscs—are used throughout the art world to enhance
exhibitions and to reach and engage audiences. Computer and imaging programs offer both comprehensive and specific, indeed personalized, access to collections, essential for professional staff as well as
diverse audiences.

Merging of Audiences

A work of art not only tells us a great deal through its presence, it is
also surrounded by information about its makers, history, culture,
and society; the economics of its creation and provenance; its
chronology, exhibition history, and bibliography; and its physical
condition and location. Collections management databases containing this kind of information are essential to the work of curators, con-
servators, registrars, exhibitions staff, museum educators, lecturers,
and writers. This same data is also the source for information provided to museum audiences so that they can create the necessary
context for viewing works of art.

One of the curious aspects of interactive multimedia programs is that they link audiences that we have traditionally regarded as distinct: the scholar and the amateur. The images and information that can be made available are of value to the specialist and the generalist alike. Digital programs containing text and visual elements, whether in computer programs, on Web sites, videodiscs, or other electronic formats can serve the random purposes of the casual museum visitor, the somewhat more focused objectives of the classroom teacher, and the very precise interests of the art historian and museum professional. Obviously, there are differences in the nature of their need for information, their intent in acquiring data, and the manner in which information is employed or applied.

Creating Context In and Through Media

Art museums are both users of new technology and repositories of content. Increasingly, museums are using interactive systems containing high-quality images and extensive information about their collections to offer the public expanded opportunities to learn about art both on- and off-site. Programs installed in the museum are often set apart from the galleries (although their location is a topic of some debate). They are intended to "recontextualize" works of art by providing more information than can be offered in an object label and by presenting it in a form that responds to the inquirer. The fluid, open-ended nature of such systems enhances the experience for the public, because it engages individuals in the act of exploring the art and in discovering ideas and relationships. Programs encourage viewers to actively seek information that bridges personal experience, knowledge, interests, and the object. Because digital images provide fidelity to the work of art and a degree of clarity that cannot be achieved in conventional media, they support and encourage close study, revealing details that may be missed, permitting exploration of the medium, and offering paths to the original work.

Authenticity of Experience

To most of us in art museums, the value of an original work of art is that it is unique, real, authentic. We are fully aware that reproductions are simply copies, and not to be confused with originals. And we worry that our audiences may not see the distinctions, that they will find a media surrogate satisfying enough to make the museum visit and encounter with the original unnecessary. Yet there is much evidence that speaks to significant public interest in art. In 1992, the National Endowment for the Arts reported that the U.S. audience for television programs on the visual arts numbered around 500 million viewers. And, from all accounts, hundreds of thousands around the world are accessing images and information about art through the electronic technologies, including numerous museum Web sites.

Clearly, these figures do not translate directly into museum visitors. Actually, only about 10 percent of a television audience visits museums. But the stimulus for those visits may come from the media. One may infer that a similar situation pertains to the "electronic" audience. Further, it has been pointed out by many in the profession that the proliferation of prints of master paintings over the centuries, from the time of the first engravings to the present, has not caused a decline in interest, appreciation, or value of the painted image. And, in examples drawn somewhat further afield, television broadcasts of sports events and dance and opera performances seem to have stimulated attendance and sparked an interest in those activities. A 1995 National Endowment of the Arts survey investigating the ages of audiences noted, however, a decline in younger audiences for classical music and opera, but did not delve into the proliferation of lesser-known, less-established, and less-expensive companies whose performances seem to elicit the enthusiasm of a "younger" audience.

In embracing media within the museum and beyond it, are we diluting the museum experience or the encounter with art? The answer, I think, is no. Media, if properly used, can enhance exhibitions, reach and engage audiences, and illuminate works of art. For example, visitor comments about the National Gallery of Art's Micro Gallery indicated that "the process of discovery, both how to use the program and finding the desired information, was a key ingredient in the pleasure people found in their experience with the program." According to a recently completed evaluation of the Micro Gallery: "Comments from those interviewed suggest they were using it as a tool either before or after visiting the galleries. There was no evidence that visitors . . . were using it as a substitute for looking at art. If anything, it was the opposite. For those who used the program before their visit, it was a way to orient themselves—an advance organizer. . . . Those who came to the Micro Gallery in the middle of or after being in the galleries used it to learn more about what they had just seen" (Science Learning, inc., 1996). Visitors also frequently remark that they would like to explore the images and information at their leisure, reserving the experience of seeing the actual work for their time in the museum. There is increasing confirmation from a variety of studies that audiences are able to differentiate between what they are experiencing through the media and the separate, but often simultaneous, experience of the art. Looking at art and looking at a media presentation are not the same thing. Nevertheless, each experience—separate or intertwined—has its own reality and is thus an "authentic" experience.

Virtual Museums: Altering the Concept of Place

Electronic imaging applications have, as noted, altered our concept of audience, creating links between traditionally disparate groups. These technologies are also changing our concept of the art museum as a place, for entire collections have become, in a sense, "portable." For example, the collections of the National Gallery in London and many other art museums have been published on CD-ROM. And a CD-ROM on the Barnes Collection in Philadelphia, for years one of the least visible collections, was produced in 1995. The latter brings into the home environment not only images but the voices and likenesses of a number of experts who comment on both the works of art and the collection. The program strives to suggest the appearance of the Barnes Collection galleries, depicting and replicating the rooms and the arrangements of the artworks. One can select any of the paintings for closer viewing and obtain additional information in text and audio. This creates not just a virtual museum but a "supra-virtual" experience, since, in the actual building, the works are not attended by the contextual commentary available in the surrogate form.

The Internet has become the primary conduit for moving the content of museums and exhibitions into homes, schools, universities, and libraries. Through on-line programs, the visual arts have become available as never before, in both in number and range of images. Museum collections, objects offered and sold at auction, and artworks presented by commercial galleries are now accessible to a worldwide public. Image banks, large and small, are being offered by more and more art museums. Works from such institutions as the National Museum of American Art, the Dallas Museum of Art, and the Louvre are all "traveling" on the information superhighway.

For reasons of speed and memory size, images are often relatively small and are intended primarily for reference use. Large image files necessary for high-resolution images are compressed and manipulated in the attempt to minimalize the download time and memory needed to transmit and store such images and also in the hopes of circumventing unauthorized use. Nevertheless, the profusion of images now accessible on-line and through other technologies is essential for supporting the study of works of art and permits comparison of multiple images from many different sources at will. The Internet, in particular, is fostering pluralism and the forging of new connections among concepts, images, disciplines, institutions, and individuals—and this is not inappropriate to the arts (*Humanities and Arts* 1994, p. 25).

There are other advantages to the ability to transport images and related contextual information: Not only does this diminish the stress on works of art engendered by physical movement, but interactive interpretative programs decrease both the distribution and production costs for reaching faraway audiences. (What must be entered into the calculation, of course, are the costs for preparing and designing the content for electronic distribution.)

Thus the new technologies are opening the walls of the art museum. Visitors may find themselves "virtually" exploring the times and places where works of art were created, conveyed conceptually to Renaissance Italy or Monet's garden at Giverny. At the same time, works of art, their contexts, and their display arrangements are being electronically transported out of our exhibit spaces to be examined and visited in homes and other settings by individuals who may never enter the art museum. Certainly, the audiences for programs available through electronic networks can be expanded considerably beyond a museum's immediate community or even prescribed constituency for outreach programs. This is particularly advantageous to smaller, perhaps lesser-known, museums, whose audiences—people who will become familiar with the museum and its collections through electronic networks—will undoubtedly exceed the institution's wildest dreams. The prospect of a student in Nanking, China, knowing about the ancient Greek vases or Roman mosaics in the collection of the Michael C. Carlos Museum in Atlanta, for example, is not out of the question. Electronic networks can create "a level playing field," so to speak. The Internet is a great equalizer among museums large and small, rural and urban, well-known and lesser-known, and among objects and their creators as well. The content transmitted through electronic networks takes up more-or-less equal space, creating innumerable opportunities for selection and choice in a fluid, non-hierarchical environment.

Our perception of place—*where* an individual sees and learns about objects and our collections—is another aspect of the conceptual change being brought about by interactive technologies. As audiences change and are reconfigured, there surely must be a related transformation in how they acquire information about objects in museum collections. Given the variations in the practices, capabilities, and facilities of school systems, it is not unthinkable that individuals will use their own means of access to find and acquire information, and look to other centers—museums, for example—to give coherence to the information obtained from the digital environment. Museums have a crucial role to play in translating information into knowledge, fostering understanding of accessible information, and in providing touchstones for the original, tangible, unique objects that constitute our collections.

Reconceptualizing the Museum and Reordering Content

The 1991 opening of the first art museum interactive information center, the Micro Gallery at the National Gallery in London, generated some very interesting and astute observations. Quite in line with expectations, many critics argued that experiencing a painting on a computer screen is an unsatisfying way of engaging with a work of art. That is true of course, but we should not confuse the two: The experience of an original work of art is surely authentic, but we cannot say that the experience of multimedia is inauthentic. It is a genuine experience; it is simply different. Critics also argued that reducing all images to the same size is in itself a distortion. We do not dispute this, but note that the same charge has been leveled for years against slides, the mainstay of the art historian, curator, and teacher! And many other visitors acknowledged the new capabilities afforded to the viewer in a Micro Gallery or in the home.

Some critics addressed the creative and iconoclastic potential of the medium; namely, that an interactive program, which offers opportunities "to step across the boundaries of national school and chronology, according to which collection[s are] arranged . . . encourages a planned defiance of the museum's own principles of organization" (Graham-Dixon 1993). This is an aspect of digital technologies that is often obscured: the inherently revolutionary—one writer called it "subversive"—element that is related to the ease with which computers can be used to reorder and rearrange; "it challenges the notion that there is only one way to structure anything" (Graham-Dixon 1993). The digital environment not only permits, but encourages, hierarchical fluidity.

The new technologies are forcing a reconceptualizing of the museum; the museum of the future has been described as a place that constantly challenges its own preconceptions of audience, place, and where and how art can be experienced. We in the art museum field, most of us art historians, argue for the primacy of the experience of the original work. But our information tells us that museum visitors tend to average only 15 to 20 seconds in front of a work of art. Thus in our search for the means to make the encounter with art more significant and more sustained, we are increasingly turning to technology to recontextualize objects, to permit both the novice and the scholar to approach works of art in new ways, to elicit new insights and, indeed, new questions. By opening our walls, our vaults, our libraries, our curatorial files electronically, we are offering the public an opportunity to reshape the museum with us. According to a 1994 report on humanities and arts programs on the World Wide Web, "Electronic technologies have the potential to transform information from a scarce, inequitably distributed, and fragmented 'commodity' into a true public good, one that is virtually inexhaustible as well as perpetually renewed and expanded" (*Humanities and Arts*

1994, p. 25). It is the potential for bringing together global content and universal access that validates the promise of new technologies not as subversive but, surely, as democratic.

References

Graham-Dixon, A. 1993. The virtual art gallery comes of age. *The Independent*, September 1993.

Humanities and arts on the information highways: A profile. 1994. Santa Monica, Calif.: The Getty Art History Information Program, The American Council of Learned Societies, The Coalition for Networked Information, September 1994.

Larrabee, Eric, ed. 1968. *Museums and education.* Washington, D.C.: Smithsonian Institution Press.

Science Learning, inc. 1996. Evaluation report, Micro Gallery, phase II. Unpublished report for the National Gallery of Art. Washington, D.C.: Science Learning, inc.

chapter 6

Digital Imaging and Issues of Authenticity in the Art Museum

Jay A. Levenson

Similar to many institutions whose missions have little to do with technology, art museums have tended either to be extremely wary of computers or to launch themselves with more enthusiasm than insight into projects involving their use. Several years ago, when CD-ROMs appeared to be the medium of the future for art publishing, a number of museums, with strong encouragement from fledgling production companies, felt compelled to rush at least one disc of their own to completion. As the market for art CD-ROMs resisted most early efforts to develop it commercially, however, that initial flurry of activity quickly ended. Production companies have become very hesitant to commit funds to costly art CD-ROMs, and museums are now hurrying instead to publish pages on the World Wide Web. Many of their existing Web sites, however, serve principally as bulletin boards—advertisements for exhibitions and other public programs—rather than as significant public resources. Most have yet to develop convincing strategies that make use of the interactive and educational possibilities of the Internet.

Computer stations set up within the museum are another very popular current use of digital technology, allowing visitors access to images of and information about the collections. These immediately give the museum an appealingly high-tech look,

Jay A. Levenson is director, International Program, the Museum of Modern Art (MoMA), New York. Trained as an art historian and as a lawyer, he organized a number of exhibitions for the National Gallery of Art, Washington, D.C., including "Circa 1492" and "The Age of the Baroque in Portugal."

although the explanatory information offered tends to be basic and is always dependent upon the amount of catalogued data the museum already has available on the objects in its collection. Still, the only damper to this particular use of digital imaging appears to be its expense: Unlike Web pages, computer stations require a considerable investment in hardware and programmers' time without any guarantee of a return from commercial use, and their development is often dependent upon finding outside sponsorship. But for that significant limitation, one has the feeling that every museum would furnish a roomful of computers to serve as its orientation center.

Sometimes opposing and often influencing these efforts to embrace information technology, however, is a countervailing mistrust of digital media on the part of some museum professionals. Many curators are perfectly content with printed publications. They seem to suspect that digital products are either not good enough when compared to their counterparts in print or, worse, are too good, in the sense that they make it easy for the computer-literate to pirate and misuse the images they contain. And within art museums themselves, there are ongoing debates over how much printed text and how many contextual images are appropriate in an exhibition context, and whether computer monitors should be placed near installations of paintings.

Part of the problem seems to involve the broader issue of authenticity. Art museums rightly view their primary role as providing their visitors the direct experience of original works of art. Their programs are supposed to serve that fundamental mission. Reproductions have their place only when they enhance this experience, either by supplying contextual information within the galleries or by allowing high-quality images to be taken home by visitors through publications.

Digital images present special cause for concern at both ends of the continuum of quality. At the current stage of their evolution, they rarely challenge the primacy of printed images in terms of fidelity to the original, and there are few curators who would replace printed catalogues with CD-ROMs, even if the public willing to purchase digital publications were large enough to support the change. Already, however, digital images have the appeal of the new. The banks of computer stations set up in well-funded institutions are often crowded with users pouring over scanned reproductions of the very works of art that can be seen in the original in adjacent galleries. Moreover, prophets of the digital age love to predict that when technologies for viewing, storing, and distributing images improve, the museum experience itself may no longer be necessary for many segments of the public. They maintain that casual museum-goers will find that digital replicas will make obsolete a visit to the museum to view the original works.

Digital Versus Print Media

There is of course no dichotomy these days between images of works of art that appear on the computer monitor and those that are viewed on a printed page; the difference is in the method of output. Both usually begin with a photographic transparency that is scanned and turned into a digital file. In a digital publication, that file is output directly to a computer monitor. In printed books the file is used to create color separations through which the image is (usually) replicated on four separate printing plates, one for each ink color used in the printing process.

However, there is a considerable difference between the two media in the degree of image resolution. Printing techniques suitable for quality art books require the use of scanners capable of creating very high-resolution files, as the printed images are delineated with screens of about 150-200 lines to the inch, each containing dots of varying size that to the unaided eye blend together on the page and appear to form areas of continuous tone.

The home computer monitor displays a much coarser matrix, which is currently standardized at 640 by 480 pixels, or dots of light, each of which is composed of varying amounts of red, green, or blue. (In most home computers each pixel is one of 256 different colors, a limitation imposed by the amount of built-in memory reserved for video, although standards are currently shifting in the direction of much larger palettes of 64,000 or 16 million colors.)

Simply put, there is much less information contained in an image that is designed to occupy a computer screen than in one that is designed to fill a printed image of the same size. (Even the highest-resolution printed page, in turn, contains much less information than the photographic transparency from which it was made.) If one were to take the file underlying a full-screen computer image on a current-generation CD-ROM and use it to print a page of the same dimensions, the individual dots comprising the image would become disturbingly evident to the naked eye.

Because of this difference in resolution most fears about the theft of digital images by outsiders with access to a museum's Web site or CD-ROM publications are, at least with present-day technologies, generally overstated. While it is relatively easy for an experienced user to "grab" a digital image from a screen display (the necessary software is actually built into the Macintosh operating system), that image consists of only one screen, generally composed of 640 by 480 pixels. If the underlying image is a larger file that requires several screens to display, the individual screens would have to be grabbed separately and then carefully pasted together to recreate the whole image. On the whole, it would be more difficult to create a quality printed reproduction by using images taken from a CD-ROM than by scanning them directly from an art book (and good-quality scanners can now be purchased for less than $1,000). Surely no museum would hesitate to publish the best possible reproduction it could create, simply because it was afraid that the image would be misappropriated by an unscrupulous purchaser; this reasoning ought to be applied to digital publishing, as well.

There is another significant but much less discussed limitation on the fidelity of images viewed on the home computer. While software and optical devices that allow a user to match the colors appearing on a given monitor to a set of standardized colors are available, these systems are generally used only within the printing industry to adjust the peculiarities of individual monitors to the printers used to output proofs. Moreover, in high-end printing a great deal of human effort is put into checking the colors of the final printed output against those of the original transparency (although, ironically, more attention appears to be paid to the color fidelity of advertising images than of those appearing in most art books). Home users generally have no tools available to correct the idiosyncrasies of their monitors in reproducing color from the files on their CD-ROMs or on the Internet.

Printed media have yet another advantage over digital publications: They can be browsed effectively by even the most casual user. It is easy to scan a series of well laid-out text labels in an exhibition and find one's area of interest, and anyone picking up a book can usually open to the right image with remarkable speed. Despite all the efforts that are being put into interface design, it now takes much more time to navigate through a CD-ROM on the same subject, the one exception being text searches, which can be carried out much more quickly through the search engine of a computer than the index of a book. And anyone with a dial-in connection to the Internet knows the frustration of waiting for images from the World Wide Web to appear on the monitor given the speed limitations of current modems and transmission techniques.

Advantages of Digital Media

Many of the visual shortcomings of digital publications will surely change when home computer monitors increase in size and resolution, and institutions presenting images on the Internet will be able to offer far larger images when faster connections become more widespread. Yet even with the current limitations, there are certain inherent advantages to viewing images of works of art on the computer screen. These include the special characteristics of the image on the screen (see below), the economy of making a large number of images available to the user, and the ease of manipulating those images. (One should not forget that in addition to these advantages in imaging—the subject of this essay—digital media offer the possibility of including sound and video in the publication, types of information that could otherwise be communicated only through film and videotape.)

The computer monitor's cathode ray tube creates a glowing image, resembling a photographic slide projected onto a beaded screen. The quality of the image is remarkably sympathetic to the luminosity of an oil painting viewed under strong light. Bright highlights emerge with a force that is difficult to replicate in a book. Other types of artworks are less suited to this type of reproduction; prints and drawings are of course most naturally replicated on the printed page.

While a full-screen image on a CD-ROM may be much

lower in resolution than a page-sized image in a large-format book, it is economically feasible to include a huge number of such images on the CD-ROM. At present, discs can easily contain more than 600 images, and improvements in compression technologies and in storage media will make it feasible to include many more. (The storage capacity of the computers used as Internet servers is much larger; the San Francisco Fine Arts Museums already offer access to about 60,000 images on their Web site). That means that on a CD-ROM or a Web site, an overall view of a painting or object can easily be supplemented with numerous details of the same work, in the case of a two-dimensional image, or with views from various angles, in the case of a three-dimensional work.

Anyone who has worked on the design of an art publication knows how difficult it can be from a production standpoint to illustrate each work with a sufficiently large images. Large color transparencies—4" x 5" or even 8" x 10"—are the medium of choice for source material, but the astonishing amount of detail contained in these photographs can rarely be captured within the size limits for illustration that are mandated by production costs. These financial constraints restrict the total number of pages of even the grandest exhibition catalogue, and written entries and scholarly footnotes are likely to take up a great deal of the available printed space. In many cases only the most significant works in a volume can receive full-page illustrations, while most others must be reproduced in far from optimal formats. Moreover, a printed publication often has to compromise on issues of scale. If the designer chooses to make all the reproductions of a single size—as is often the case with books that place a page of text opposite a full-page illustration—small objects may be magnified out of all proportion to their real dimensions.

Digital media, on the other hand, can contain numerous details of a work or even reproduce the work in several files of successively higher resolution. A small object can be shown initially as a small-scale screen image. The program can then allow the user to jump from an area on the first screen image to the corresponding area of a second higher-resolution image, giving the effect of magnifying that detail. If there is enough disk space, several successive magnifications can be offered, with the highest conveying a real sense of the surface texture of the painting or object.

There are particular advantages in digital technology for the imaging of three-dimensional works. Reproducing these objects in books often requires considerable compromise. Only a photographer of real knowledge and skill, working with knowledgeable advice from a scholar, can choose the view that best does justice to a work of sculpture or other object in the round. With some originals no single viewpoint is really satisfactory. A CD-ROM can easily include multiple views of an object. There are even means of providing the illusion of looking at the work in the round, although at present these offer lower-resolution images than single views. For example, a videotape of the work rotating on a turntable can be inserted into a CD-ROM. Apple's QuickTime VR software allows a series of still photographs of an object taken from different angles to be integrated into a single wrap-around view, allowing the user to rotate the object at will. The same technology also allows for a "virtual" experience of a show. The viewer is able to place himself at any of several locations within an exhibition gallery, pivot 360 degrees to scan the walls of the room, and even, to a limited extent, appear to approach the objects, which grow in size as the visitor gets closer.

While "virtual reality" on the desktop computer is still a relatively primitive affair, high-powered work stations, now far too expensive for casual use, can provide a more convincing experience. ENEL, the Italian state energy company, has sponsored a series of virtual-reality recreations of famous art sites which give a sense of the future of this approach. The spaces—such as the basilica of St. Peter's in Rome, the ancient tomb of Queen Nefertari in Egypt's Valley of Kings, Raphael's *Stanze* in the Vatican, or the basilica in Assisi with its frescoes by Giotto—are rendered in three dimensions, and the wall surfaces are reproduced from detailed transparencies. A simple joystick with an intuitive interface allows the user to look at the surroundings from any angle and roam through the spaces at will, in some cases with the option of elevating himself to any position within the spatial envelope. The immense processing power of the work station makes the pace of this journey approach or exceed a real-time tour. Until recently, only a single resolution image could be included in the program for each surface. Thus, if the user moved towards the image of a fresco on a wall, the corresponding digital image would simply be enlarged by the program and would ultimately begin to look fuzzy and undefined. A new generation of virtual-reality work stations allow several images of successively higher resolution to be accessed, so that as one advances towards a wall surface, the program shifts imperceptibly from one digital file to the next: The image of the fresco on the wall seems to grow not only larger, but also sharper.

Issues of Authenticity

Digital publications, then, are most effective when they are unlike books, when they are used in ways that exploit the advantages of digital imaging and overcome the limitations of replicating works of art on the printed page. Thus new media can address the difficulties of reproducing three-dimensional objects in two dimensions by including multiple views; they can suggest the space and architecture that surround monumental works of art through the techniques of virtual reality; and they can allow a user to access vast quantities of images—far more than any museum could afford to publish in print—quickly and economically through digital storage technologies.

Yet art museums that have begun to make use of digital media have concentrated their resources almost exclusively on products that resemble books, such as CD-ROM versions of exhibition catalogues. These are often little more than computerized editions of printed publications, up-to-date in their technology but relentlessly old-fashioned in their organization and content. Moreover, it is precisely this type of project that suffers most from the limitations of current technology, due to the fact that an image viewed on the average monitor is much lower in resolution and less faithful to the color of the original than a carefully printed image of equivalent size.

Even the digital databases of museum collections that have been made available to the public—whether designed to be accessed in the museum through kiosks or at home on CD-ROMs or via the Internet—are of limited benefit for most audiences. The idea of publishing all of an institution's works on disk initially sounds very appealing. In most cases, however, such projects address only the needs of the specialist, who requires access to images of every last work in a museum's storeroom. Museums have yet to develop the type of cooperative project that promises useful results for the general public. A CD-ROM with images of all the prints of Rembrandt, regardless of collection, is of far greater utility to most audiences than a database of all the prints in a particular museum's collection, regardless of artist.

Moreover, when museums do not turn directly to printed books as models for their CD-ROMs, they often take their inspiration from other familiar sources, such as videos and slide lectures. Film clips and sound tracks are often integrated into CD-ROMs to accompany the flow of digitized images. It is revealing to note that a truly innovative program like the "Virtual Raphael Stanze" can be seen at Epcot Center, an entertainment complex, but not at any of the museums in this country that own original works by Raphael.

Costs and the availability of funds, of course, place limits on museums' ambitions. CD-ROM versions of printed catalogues are much cheaper to produce than virtual-reality simulations. Nevertheless, I doubt that economic limitations alone can account for this channeling of new media into well-worn paths. Long-standing concerns about authenticity also appear to play a significant role. Museums regard their primary function as facilitating the visitor's direct, even unmediated, experience of the original work of art. Books have long been a tried and true vehicle for that process, and museums will often place copies of exhibition catalogues in public galleries, encouraging the visitor to read them on the spot. More intrusive media, such as graphics and photographic images, or more seductive media, such as music, have always been suspect.

There are still no accepted standards regarding the amount of explanatory material that should accompany an art museum installation, even one of works from distant historical periods that by their nature require explication for most visitors. Tensions between artwork and explanation are evident in many exhibition galleries. Some museums print labels that are difficult to read from a distance; if the texts are larger in point size, they are likely to be severely limited in length. Ancillary photographs, such as images of the artist and reproductions of works that could not be included in the show, are often restricted to introductory or side galleries that do not contain original works of art.

In a way the issues raised by digital media are no different from the problems long posed for the art museum by physical replicas. Although in the 19th century plaster casts of famous ancient and Renaissance monuments were in extensive use, attitudes have since changed, perhaps because of the widespread availability of photographs of these works. Some museums, particularly those fortunate enough to have secure sources of income, long shunned three-dimensional reproductions altogether, even refusing to sell them in their bookstores. They worried that such objects would dilute the visitor's experience by undercutting the centrality of the original work of art. Books and other two-dimensional images, including elaborately-framed reproductions of paintings, were thought to be acceptable, since they were so clearly designed to be illustrations rather than replicas. Over time, the need of most museums to supplement their incomes through sales brought three-dimensional facsimiles to virtually all bookstores (now renamed "shops"), but the distrust remained. Replicas are today rarely found within the exhibition galleries; they are regarded as suitable only for takeout.

On the other hand, history and science museums, as well as libraries, have always had a quite different attitude toward reproductions and facsimiles. These institutions regard the intellectual structure of their exhibitions, not the objects, as primary. They often include facsimiles in displays when the originals are not readily obtainable. No curator of paleontology would omit the Jurassic from a presentation of the development of dinosaurs simply because the particular museum's collections were weak in works of that period. Instead he or she makes the point with replicas or photographs.

Not surprisingly, digital media are much more in evidence in natural history museums and libraries than in art museums. Multimedia kiosks play a featured role in, to take one example, the latest dinosaur installations, which often employ such extensive didactic materials that at times the fossils themselves seem in danger of being overwhelmed by the explanatory texts. (In fact, curators of paleontology might do well to look to art museum installations for ideas about how to convey the uniqueness of objects to visitors).

Art museum curators, on the other hand, are so wedded to the centrality of the work of art that they are willing to sacrifice significant issues of content if a particular original is not available. An example from my own experience as managing curator of the

National Gallery of Art's exhibition "Circa 1492: Art in the Age of Exploration" makes this point clear. Unlike most art museum exhibitions, this show dealt with a theme from world history rather than art history. It commemorated the Columbus quincentennial by presenting a view of the major civilizations of the late 15th-century world through the works of art that they produced. Major secular works from the late Middle Ages have survived in very limited numbers and, as a result, there were a number of cases where a particular point of the show's thesis could be made only if a particular work of art could be borrowed.

One of these unique objects was a darkened, leather-covered globe preserved in the Germanisches Nationalmuseum in Nuremberg, a work famous to cartographers but not especially well-known outside their field. Created on the orders of Martin Behaim—a member of one of Nuremberg's patrician families who worked for the Portuguese court in Lisbon and probably learned about the "Enterprise of the Indies" directly from Columbus—the object was completed in 1492. It is the earliest preserved terrestrial globe, and it depicts a readily recognizable Europe and Africa, with fanciful outlines for the coast of Asia, which was known to Behaim principally from the description in Marco Polo's narrative. Documents in the Nuremberg archives indicate that the globe was paid for by the city government. One theory is that Behaim designed it and had it produced for a fund-raising presentation to local financiers in an effort to bankroll a rival expedition to Columbus's.

Once painted a bright blue, the globe darkened considerably at some point in the 19th century after an unsuccessful attempt at restoration. It had become so dark, in fact, that when I saw it in Nuremberg I wondered whether we should even consider including it in an exhibition in which the objects were supposed to be as beautiful as they were meaningful. As I stood in the room, however, two teenagers walked up to the globe, circled it quickly, and immediately grasped its significance. "Look," one said, "no America!" It is rare that an an object communicates a point—that educated Europeans knew the world was round before they knew that America existed—so directly and with such concreteness. Moreover, the globe had been decorated by a leading illuminator; it was arguably a work of art as well as a historical document.

Unfortunately, the curator in Nuremberg responsible for the globe could not imagine its ever leaving the museum, and there were real questions about whether the work could be safely transported. After more than a year's negotiation, I realized that the cause was hopeless. There would have been no point in showing a photograph, as the special significance of the Behaim globe can only be perceived in three dimensions; one has to be able to walk around it to understand it. There were, however, several full-scale three-dimensional facsimiles of the globe that had been created in the late-19th century, one of them owned by the Smithsonian, and our curatorial team had to decide whether to include one of them. If we left out the facsimile, we would lose the chance to make an important intellectual point. Yet the National Gallery has a policy against displaying reproductions in its exhibitions, and in every other case that arose we had decided against including facsimiles.

There were cogent reasons not to include the reproduction. It was not an exact representation of the globe in its current state; it attempted instead to reconstruct its original 15th-century appearance. The sea was painted bright blue (probably based on remnants of the original paint that were still visible), and many of the finer details of the cartography were omitted or coarsened in the reproduction. While it gave a general idea of the original, it misrepresented the real globe's aesthetic qualities, and it arguably did not belong in an exhibition in which the selection of works depended precisely on those qualities.

Still, most history museums or libraries would have displayed the facsimile of the Behaim globe without any hesitation, and some, in fact, did during that quincentennial year. Until I began writing this chapter, I never doubted that the decision to omit the facsimile was correct. In retrospect, I think that for "Circa 1492," Behaim's globe was such a necessary object that merely describing and illustrating it in the exhibition catalogue, as we did, was insufficient. There were surely many visitors who passed through the show without realizing that such an object existed in 1492. One solution would have been to include a facsimile, clearly marked as such and separated from the original objects. Another possibility, much more feasible now than at the time of the exhibition (1991), would have been to create a digitized replica of the globe accessible on a computer kiosk.

The Behaim globe is not an isolated example of this type of dilemma. Paintings and carvings of the Paleolithic period in Europe and Africa begin every written survey of the history of art, and yet even the most encyclopedic museum in this country starts its presentation with the art of Egypt and Mesopotamia. The reason is that the original Paleolithic works belong to a relatively small number of European and African institutions, most of them ethnographic or natural history museums, and can no longer be acquired nor, under normal circumstances, borrowed. Natural history museums may include an entire room of facsimiles of such objects in their presentations of prehistory. Yet art museums regularly omit this first chapter of the history of art from their galleries because the originals are unavailable. Perhaps the Lascaux and Altamira caves, like Behaim's globe and Raphael's *Stanze*, are also appropriate candidates for virtual reality renderings.

This is not to suggest that museums should shift their focus from the display of original works of art to the computerized reconstructions of unobtainable masterpieces. Digital publications, like books, should always play a subsidiary role in the art museum, as tools for explanation rather than as ends in themselves. Properly used, they will not compete for visitors' attention with the original works of art. Digital imaging will be of greatest utility for the museum, however, when those responsible for its use realize that the medium's special strengths should define the applications it creates inside the museum, whether on kiosks, CD-ROMs, or the Internet. The computer is a logical means to access comprehensive and well-organized databases of images. It is also a valuable tool for conveying information about objects that are difficult to photograph, especially three-dimensional sculpture and works of art that are part of larger architectural ensembles. At present, when properly used, digital media effectively complement rather than compete with the printed publications that they will some day—when display technologies improve—almost certainly replace.

chapter 7

Networked Media: The Experience Is Closer than You Think

Stephen Borysewicz

As museums continue to create greater opportunities for informal public learning, many museum professionals are eager to make museum resources available to visitors through the various forms of new media. We're all aware of the continued growth of public access to new media. Yet it sometimes seems that the steady increase in the number of networked computer users and the continued introduction of hardware and software innovations has had a restraining effect on content providers; the constant "newness" of the media makes us reluctant to commit to learning new skills and assigning resources that, in museums, are already spread pretty thin. But the rate of growth is not as important as the number of people who already use computer networks, CD-ROMs, videoconferencing, and other communications tools on a daily basis. That number is already far too large for us to ignore.

But what museum content should we make available through the World Wide Web, CD-ROMs, and live video hook-ups? And what model should we use for creating that content? The same content presented in exhibits can serve well in other media without competing with its source: the actual museum. While working on exhibits and networked media programs, I found some acutely delineated affinities between the development of conventional exhibits

Stephen Borysewicz was a native of Chicago. For many years he was an exhibit developer at the Field Museum of Natural History, Chicago, where he worked on a number of exhibits, including "Life Over Time." He also initiated the museum's Web site. He died on Aug. 24, 1997, at the age of 39.

and the development of content in new media, specifically programs delivered over computer networks. Recognizing these affinities can help us use electronic media to support the museum's role as a venue for viewing authentic objects, enjoying powerful affective experiences, and social interaction.

I'm in an enormous, world-famous museum, and I'm looking at a computer screen filled with charming images. After a moment, I realize that some of them are active; if I click the cursor on certain icons, I'll get information about particular paintings and sculpture from the museum's collection. I experiment for a while, clicking, trying to figure out how to get back to the original screen, waiting for images to load, wondering what it is exactly that certain icons are asking me to do. I wish I could sit down. After I walk away, I find a painting that interests me. I wish the computer was nearby to provide me with more information than I can get from a label.

In the earliest days of the World Wide Web, museums posted new home pages at an impressive rate, taking a lead in creating coherent, useful content for researchers and the public. Sometimes program developers, educators or curators initiated the creation of programming. But in many cases librarians, archivists, or museum informatics staff—those people most experienced with computerized storage and retrieval of large numbers of data—were the first to bring this new "morph" of content delivery to their museums. Over the years, a number of models were attempted, all with some degree of success. From those highly individualistic and forward-thinking beginnings, we now see decisions about on-line content being made (or debated or postponed) in committee, which is the more natural way for complex institutions to function.

It is now possible for every museum, not to mention all for-profit and nonprofit institutions and every individual with the time and money, to become a multimedia content provider. Tools for creating programming and the expertise to use them are ubiquitous. At the same time, the world of globally networked communications remains decisively in flux, guaranteeing a continuing flood of prognostications, forecasts, trend analyses . . . and increased access, too.

And while entrepreneurs acclimate themselves to the new terminology of the computer industry, learning to describe themselves as being in the media business rather than the technology business, while marketers race to position their clients' products and names in the consumer and business press—museums are forging ahead, delivering highly educational, interactive informal content to an eager public. Museum exhibit developers can be confident that the exhibit practices they've honed during the past half-century will serve them well in the still-expanding and wonderfully vague venue of new media.

Creation of computer-based programming does not involve the same construction and maintenance costs of exhibit production, but it is still relatively costly. We already are accustomed to the expenses of video and audio production. We understand the costs involved in the creation of a three-dimensional gallery space with artifacts, models, graphics, and interactives. But while software and hardware will continue to be the least expensive portions of an on-line program's budget, the development costs of new media remain high. The development of any media program will consume the vast portion of its budget.

Interactive Media and Museum Content Are a Good Fit

It's fairly simple to answer the question of what type of content is appropriate for a museum Web site, CD-ROM, or other media product intended for public learning. Museum exhibit spaces are venues for informal learning and social interaction. Obviously, the World Wide Web and other electronic media are relevant channels for the distribution of programming designed for informal learning and social enjoyment, too. For museums, the Web fulfills this role in a number of useful ways:

- Content can be controlled by the developer (museum) and accessed directly by users, without the mediation of a middleman such as a publisher.
- The line between entertainment and education is blurred on the Web, just as it is increasingly in museums.
- Users can locate content through term searches (resolving the "I didn't know this museum had that painting" syndrome).
- Computer networks typically function as meeting grounds for people, just as museums do.

- Museums already have a sophisticated and useful model for creating multimedia experiences that translates readily to new media.

Creating New Media Programming Should Be a Familiar Process

As I learned how to create World Wide Web and CD-ROM programs, I was awed and at the same time disappointed by the technology. I expected a lot more in some areas than was possible (especially in image quality and speed of access), but was amazed by the breadth of media and interaction that were available. Eventually, I realized that I was thinking just like an exhibit developer, which finally opened my eyes to the real possibilities for enriched communication with a museum audience.

Once we start matching some key components of the museum visit with characteristics of electronic media, we can see the potential for addressing a museum audience through computer and other programs.

Social environment. Museums are already accustomed to constructing environments based on an understanding of their visitors' social behavior. During visiting hours, we hope that the public spaces of our museums are populated and that our audience feels rewarded for spending time with us. We've become very sophisticated about what that reward might be; we know that it's the audience, not our own evaluation of our content offering, that defines the value of a museum experience. With this knowledge, we create exhibits that are great places where people can interact not only with the content but with each other.

A 19th-century illustration (figure 1) elicits some wonderfully sharp observations: How many visitors are actually looking at the shells, the stuffed giraffe, the swooping hammerhead shark? How many people are looking at, talking to, or flirting with one another? But from the fun everybody is having, is it likely that these people didn't feel that their visit to the gallery was worthwhile?

People do go to museums to look, but they go for lots of other reasons, too. People connect to networks to look, but they also connect for other, extremely compelling reasons. Watch a group of

Figure 1. 19th-century illustration of people doing everything we don't expect them to at a museum. Courtesy The Field Museum, Chicago, #GN87692.03c. Photo by John Weinstein.

children as they work at a single computer together, or communicate with one another via computer, and you'll see the same social dynamic that's acted out in public, theme-oriented spaces. Take your laptop to the laundromat, and kids will ask you if you've got an Internet connection and whether they can look at the Web.

On my lunch hour, I sit at my computer, prowling the Web for new resources. I'm not sure how, but I stumble onto a site that archives theme songs from hundreds of television shows going back the early 1950s. The site was created by a private individual; there's no indication that copyright laws have been observed. Yet I can choose to download any of hundreds of audio files, all carefully categorized by type of show. Within minutes, my cubicle is full of coworkers demanding to hear their favorite songs, and intense discussions about old T.V. shows begin. Soon, as a group, we're searching the Web for pages that display images, scripts, cast lists, and sound bites of dialogue.

Technology. People visit museums with the expectation that they'll be given access to new technologies. In the 1950s, the queen of England could see herself on color television at Chicago's Museum of

Figure 2. The queen of England goes to a museum to see herself on color television. Courtesy Stephen Borysewicz.

Science and Industry (figure 2). Governments and businesses continue to underwrite technology-based museum exhibits to educate the public and promote their own agendas. And exhibitors attempt to keep up with the latest technology, experimenting with ways to include it in our exhibits and keep them "relevant."

Computer networks are terrific at delivering sensational, timely subject matter. The National Aeronautics and Space Administration (NASA) provided a live World Wide Web link to the space shuttle way back in 1994! And network users rely on the network itself as a supplier of new technology and news about that technology. Infrequent and inexperienced users are justifiably intimidated by the steepness of the learning curve in networked media, but veteran users place high value on that continual learning process.

Mystery and wonder. At museums, people immerse themselves in the exploration of mysteries, scrutinizing and interacting with objects that are profoundly different from things they encounter in everyday life. Museums have become familiar to much of the public for their temporary exhibits of new discoveries; in the late '60s and early '70s, exhibits on the U.S. space program were a big draw, such as the moon rocks—holy relics of the space program—displayed at Chicago's Field Museum (figure 3). Permanent, less sensational displays have a more individualized effect, but they can confound or provoke for a lifetime; stuffed wild animals, mummies, artworks, and dinosaurs are eternal stimuli of atavistic compulsions.

Museum visitors also explore immersive environments. But visiting a reconstructed old European village street, ancient coal forest, or African savannah constitutes an experience that's only partially educational by any test. Many on-line environments, especially those created by imaginative individuals, are equally exotic, in the way that a walk-through diorama tries to be. This immersion in computer space requires a shift in paradigm; the metaphor of physical space is not appropriate. Computer space is energized and made complex through graphics, multimedia links, hidden messages, and navigational choices. On countless home pages,

Figure 3. Moon rocks, just in. Where else but a museum would we go to see the latest discovery? Courtesy The Field Museum, Chicago, #GN81799.16c.

the concept of making one's life into an artwork and inviting others in has never been realized by so many individuals so successfully. Hyperlinks take us down a myriad of rabbit holes, connecting us to information we'd just as soon not know about, but also bringing us real-time images and sounds from previously inaccessible places. Exotica so permeates the Web that it becomes almost mundane.

Memories. Many museum-goers expect to be able to revisit familiar exhibits that constitute a visible and unchangeable part of their personal construct of knowledge. These are the visitors who are disappointed at the removal of an unwrapped mummy, aghast at the rehabilitation of a fossil exhibit, and profoundly disoriented by the repositioning of a famous painting. Though it has been around for decades, the Internet is so mutable that we haven't seen loyalty to particular resources develop with quite the same fervor. (Unfortunately, at museums and on-line, it is those people whose experiences are most strongly mediated by nostalgia who seem most strident about the maintenance of a remembered learning context, sometimes at the cost of better access for others.) Current tastes for retrograde forms of entertainment may stimulate the growth of a pool of "traditional" or "historic" resources on-line. We already have access to Web sites that give users a nostalgic look at early computer games like Pong and Pac-Man, complete with wistful comparisons to the capabilities of the current 64-bit technology.

Interactivity. As a learning tool and a means of enhancing the visitor's affective experience, interactive installations are immensely valuable, if somewhat problematic in many applications. Yet many visitors expect to be allowed to interact with exhibits. The nature of electronic media encourages interactive programming, too, and many of the interactive installations we create for exhibits are easily translated into computer-modeled analogs. And on a computer network the relationships of time and audience shift in favor of the user: There's no one waiting behind you in line, and you can take as long as you like to explore a complex problem.

Challenges of Architecture

As we compare an actual museum visit and to the use of a multimedia computer program, we're naturally obliged to look at the differences, too. Certainly, there are many ways in which a World Wide Web site or CD-ROM might seem less fulfilling than a museum visit.

When we visit a museum, it's usually during the day. We're alert, our eyes and minds open, ready for anything. We've probably made some effort to actually get to the museum, so we really are looking forward to what the exhibits have to offer. We're excited by the promise the architecture holds out to us (figures 4 and 5). The landscape, an imposing facade, a brilliantly lit atrium furnished with carefully placed oversized objects all suggest that we're about to have a really important experience. Movement through architectural space, even a dysfunctional one, is a kinesthetic experience affecting most of our senses. The opportunities for manipulation seem limitless, from color to air temperature to size.

Compare that array of stimulating cues with those presented by a computer or video terminal (figure 6). Chances are we sit at our computers late at night or during the lunch hour. Whatever the time of day, we haven't made a special effort to get to the machine; it's one of our routine array of appliances. A beige plastic box, a gummy keyboard, and a screen the size of an unfolded cocktail napkin squat on a cluttered work space. If we've set ourselves up like most people do, the ergonomic relationship of the keyboard, screen, mouse, and chair are pretty unpleasant, too.

Booting up a CD-ROM or connecting to the Web requires nothing more than a series of small physical gestures—no drama, but lots of patience. Most network media delivery systems lack the visual and spatial cues that prepare museum visitors for what they hope will be a powerful affective experience. As we explore the means of translating actual, three-dimensional experiences into a two-dimensional medium, we have to dig a little deeper to find out how to give computer users the same sense of delight that's promised by the museum environment. In fact, electronic media of a certain scale usually have the effect of draining impact from most visual resources. The excitement has to come from a different context.

Actual exhibits rely on the presentation of real objects and phenomena as a fundamental part of the visitor experience. Authentic dinosaur bones, real high-voltage arcs, genuine Impressionist paintings—it's hard to imagine a computer program or video about one of those items that can impart the same thrill as the real thing. For computer-based media programs, images are only the beginning. To achieve a powerful effect, they must draw on other strengths, such

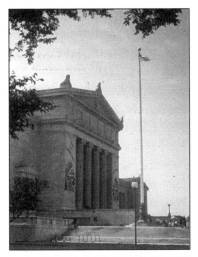

Figures 4 and 5. Architecture cues us when all else fails: We're about to have a big experience by going in here. Courtesy The Field Museum, Chicago. #GN87301.10c (Figure 4), #GEO85826c (Figure 5). Photos by John Weinstein.

Figure 6. The typical computer-user environment: ugly, cramped, and late at night. Not conducive to wonder. Courtesy Stephen Borysewicz.

as computer models, access to in-depth data resources (including video and sound files), and interactive communications links.

On its Web site, the National Library of Medicine publishes images obtained from full-color scans of a frozen human cadaver. Linked to this site are almost a dozen other sites that are working with this anatomical resource, including one that displays three-dimensional fly-throughs of the human body, reconstructed from digitized whole-body section data. At my computer, I finally begin to understand how organs, bones, and muscles are packed inside the body. Later, I visit Chicago's Museum of Science and Industry to take another look at their pickled, stained cadaver slices. The impact is entirely different. Pressed between yellowing acrylic panes, these grayish and dusky purple slabs are impressive because they're real; I'm looking inside an authentic cadaver. I note that the heart is smaller, the liver larger, than I would have thought. But I have trouble reassembling this stack of decidedly dead-looking slices of flesh into a moving, breathing human.

Computers can often induce a strong feeling of solitude, recalling the empty wings of larger or less heavily visited museums or the experience of looking at and interacting with an exhibit's content. This feeling of private, self-directed exploration, of being alone in a crowd, is cherished by many museum visitors. Clearly, that experience is replicated on-line; a network user may access a Web site at the same time as hundreds of other people and have no sense of their presence at all. The architecture of media programming is likewise invisible or obscure; users sometimes have a feeling of being lost or out of control, simply because the program they're using lacks a rational conceptual map.

Fatigue affects museum visitors and media users alike. In exhibits, we can plan for fatigue: We know we've got our visitors for a while, so here and there we give them a break by varying the density of content and providing a bathroom and a comfortable place to rest. In electronic media, the problem is a little more difficult to solve. On-line users rarely stay with a single Web site for very long; download and access times have a way of turning users to the next site after just a few minutes. But this behavior is changing, as Web designers begin to develop a better understanding of their medium's limits. CD-ROM production has its own challenges; interface design and speed of access are critical in this medium.

What Do We Do Next?

Museums are now part of a very crowded computer media world; research and experimentation by universities, designers, artists, and hardware and software companies are producing important work at a breakneck pace. But museums' special talent for creating conceptually coherent, thematically interactive multimedia programs gives us a tremendous advantage in new media production. Once we understand the new media user's context in the same way we understand the museum visitor's context, we will be able to expand our audiences and take our programs into homes and schools with relative ease.

Create a continuous, open-ended dialogue. Successful museum exhibits can compel a dialogue among visitors and between the visitor and the exhibit content. Ideally, this dialogue is open-ended; visitors add our content to their own knowledge base, adjusting it to their personal context, and go on to raise questions of their own. In reality, the long-term effects of exhibits are very difficult to track. We rarely have the opportunity to check on what people say about our programs or how long our content resides in our visitors' memories.

Networked computers facilitate this form of dialogue wonderfully. The "talk-back" units that are such a popular part of so many exhibits on controversial subjects have an exact analog in electronic bulletin boards and on-line chat rooms. For many network users, interaction with other people on-line is a core experience. And networked communications simplify maintenance of long-term dialogue within groups of virtually unlimited size and follow-up studies as well.

Let our visitors make their own museums. "Official" museums share Web space with thousands of personal museums, created by individuals interested in sharing their own versions of connoisseurship and interpretation. Often a personal museum is simply an on-line archive of an enthusiast's collection; many of these on-line collections are thorough beyond belief, and painstakingly documented. The more interesting sites express unique, highly idiosyncratic views of history and culture.

These personal museums cannot be ignored. We're all working in the same venue, stripped of many of the signifiers that cue visitors to accept one point of view as the more considered and sophisticated. When identical tools are available to all users, scholarship, elaborate graphic design, even superbly functional interface design will no longer designate "authority." We're seeing extraordinary steps being taken by anonymous individuals to ensure that they are heard and understood. This egalitarian aspect of new media should encourage us to view content as the most important determinant of utility and appeal.

It's late, and I'm checking a self-titled "virtual library" for new, interesting Web sites. Someone from Finland has posted an elaborate, comprehensive site detailing the contents of what I hope is the world's largest collection of banana brand stickers. This site has historic depth, as well as an international focus. Stickers are presented by country of sale, and users can trace the evolution of familiar icons on favorite brands. Another on-line museum documents the last run of a steam locomotive through the central Appalachians. The curator, an obvious train buff, has included audio clips and still images captured as the train rumbled over bridges and through small towns. The text describes the event in detail; the curator intends to ensure that this historic event will not pass undocumented.

Safe handling of artifacts. Exhibitors are always looking for ways to allow people to handle artifacts, take them apart, turn them upside-down, try them on. Electronic media greatly facilitate this interaction through the use of computer models. Granted, not all of the senses are served equally by computer-built and controlled models, but digital interactives are durable and can be as simple or complex as their makers desire.

Exchange objects with our public. A key feature of World Wide Web browsers is the ability to copy and save data files. As users become more educated about the potential for collecting material from the Web, museums can encourage this behavior by offering specific items as the foundation of a personal collection. We also can offer templates for constructing personalized on-line exhibits, with links to resources to help develop individual sites. Museums should be interested in showing their public the meaning of curation and the importance of systematic collecting. With the Web, we finally have a way to invite our visitors to replicate these activities and better understand our purpose and process.

Museums also can accept data files from their on-line visitors as contributions to an exhibit or as study material. Freed from restrictions on exhibit and storage space, curators and exhibit developers can find out what network users would like to see interpreted on-line. Donors take great pride in seeing their former property installed as part of a museum exhibit; using donated data can have the same effect.

Repeated visits are easy. Once an investment in hardware and network access is made, the cost to users for repeated visits to a site stays extremely low. And users respond very favorably to sites that exhibit constantly changing, updated content. Those of us who've worked at large institutions are aware of the "there's too much to see" complaint from visitors on a once-in-a-lifetime excursion. Web sites and CD-ROMs, too, can seem overwhelmingly complex. But, with interactive electronic media, any number of visits are possible. On Web sites with large databases, navigational aids can direct users to different content areas on successive visits, keeping the site fresh and encouraging users to explore.

Ownership. The more access our public has to the fundamental processes of museum work, the greater will be their sense of ownership. Museums need to be able to respond to their visitors directly, to make them feel confident that they are being heard. In actual exhibits, this kind of active response can be almost impossible. On-line programs can request contributions from their users and allow users to construct their own content or interact with the museum directly.

A European museum exists only on a Web site, its "collection" constructed exclusively of content contributed by Web site visitors. Content relating to one topic is requested; text, sound, and images are all accepted. Each time I revisit the site, it has grown. To whom does this museum belong: the users, the makers, the curators?

Browsing Equals Grazing

The affective experience of interacting with a computer program is more subtle than the experience of walking through the highly charged space of an exhibit. The new media's affective reward seems to obtain more from the discovery process and the opportunity to manipulate content than from design effects. Yet browsing through a

CD-ROM or a Web site is strikingly similar to the "grazing" behavior that museum visitors engage in—moving from attractor to attractor, not always adhering to the programmed march exhibit designers intend for them. Web sites and CD-ROMs that are developed with this behavior in mind are certain to be more successful. The same ideal of a layered content interpreted for many learning styles that applies to exhibits applies to electronic media, too.

Museum exhibitors work in a dichotomous milieu; museums can be extremely conservative environments financially, physically, and conceptually. Limitations on funding, a diversity of opinions about what constitutes the best use of exhibit resources, and constraints imposed by architecture compel us to respond cautiously to many challenges. At the same time, we are among the most experimental of all groups working with media, and one of the few groups that cares to develop a thorough understanding of an audience's behavior before imposing a program on them. Museum exhibits may be one of the only true multimedia experiences available to the public at a low cost. We ask a lot from our visitors; they have to make all sorts of arrangements to be able to spend time with us. But exhibits are one of the few public resources that are intended for group interaction, organized around both affective and cognitive experiences, and combine the excitement of learning with social, aesthetic, and imaginative rewards.

As exhibitors, we should regard new media, particularly the World Wide Web, as a resource that more closely resembles a museum visit than a museum collection. Creating programming with this characteristic in mind will enable us to bring effective, engaging museum content to a public unconstrained by geographic and temporal limitations. We already have the tools, including a familiarity with content design, script writing, and navigational planning. We already have an immense respect for user context, an understanding of the psychology of learning, and an educational mission that's adaptable to the changing needs of an extremely diverse audience. And we already support a tradition of experimentation for and responsiveness to a public that continues to choose to museums as the venue for its most compelling cultural experiences.

chapter 8

Designing Hybrid Environments: Integrating Media into Exhibition Space

Robert J. Semper

Museums use media in many different ways. In many cases, such as publishing, broadcasting, and classes, media is used in ways where standard media design principles hold. But when one introduces media into public exhibition spaces, the design rules for its production often must be reexamined. To design effective media experiences for exhibitions, one must understand the unique features of public spaces.

The Nature of Public Space

When examining media from a public space point of view, it helps to start with a review of the features of public space that can affect design.

The public space experience is three-dimensional and spatial. The media we build for public spaces should reflect space as well as content. The relationship between the space and the objects in it—the entire environment—is very important. Public environments are

Robert J. Semper is executive associate director of the Exploratorium, San Francisco. He also serves as head of the Exploratorium's new Center for Media and Communication, which is developing media for the museum and remote audiences.

Portions of this chapter are based on a paper by Robert J. Semper and Kristina Woolsey, originally presented at the first International Conference on Hypermedia and Interactivity in Museums (ICHIM), October 1991, Pittsburgh, and published in Hypermedia and Interactivity in Museums, *edited by David Bearman (Archives and Museum Informatics, 1991).*

three-dimensional, visually and aurally all-encompassing, and dynamic.

Good media design should respond to this inherent spatiality. Museum exhibit space is not a living room, classroom, theater, or office, and the media design rules, interface design, and A/V equipment that work for those environments will not necessarily work for museums. We need to think beyond the 20" cathode-ray tube to large-screen projections, multiple-image systems, and non-screen media, to create spatial media experiences that are integrated into the exhibit space.

The public space experience happens in a real place. A museum is not a broadcast medium; it's a location medium. It involves being in a place, sometimes a very specific place. People go to a particular location for its experience. For example, they visit art museums because of the specific works of art they display. The place—the Louvre, Museum of Modern Art, American Museum of Natural History—is a critical feature of the experience.

When we think about designing media for public space, we should be conscious of the potential synergistic relationship between place and media. The design of media for a museum space should carry the personality of the place itself, unlike most media, which is designed to be placeless. For projects that involve the Internet, the fact that museums exist in a specific place provides them with a distinct identity advantage over more virtual locations.

The public space experience is profoundly social. Whether one is in a museum or at a street corner waiting for a bus, one interacts with people—often with family and friends, but sometimes with strangers. The exhibit and media experience in museums often prompts discussions between visitors. In fact, the exhibits often serve as props for a conversation. Good media design (like good exhibit design) recognizes this social activity by providing space for more than one person to get involved. Successful media projects are often the ones that are accessible to more than a few people at a time.

The public space experience is non-linear. In a museum, people browse with their feet; they go where they want, do what they want, and there are all kind of factors that impact those decisions. As a designer, you may want people to go to a specific place in a particular order, but if someone is already standing at a display, a visitor will go somewhere else. Visitors navigate by spatial cues. They get a visual take on the overall experience and then decide where to go. People's behavior in museums is more like sightseeing or window shopping than reading or touring.

This non-linear experience can come into conflict with media productions, which are often linear in design and intent. It is critical to give the visitor more control over the experience than one might in more traditional media venues. Besides the obvious (but often not implemented) approach of giving people the chance to stop as well as start a media presentation, it is also a good idea to provide some information about the length, structure, and content of what is being presented. An overview provides some broad boundaries for the presentation, which helps give visitors control of their own experiences.

In public space environments learning is supported by the ability to make meaningful choices. An exhibit or media design should permit choices that are useful, interesting, and/or meaningful. There is a fine line between an approach that is too directive and one that offers such an open-ended experience that people become frustrated and lost. In good exhibit design, the material is mediated just enough to offer visitors a chance to investigate it and derive some answers, but not so much that they're given information without the opportunity to make interesting choices.

Given the physical, three-dimensional nature of exhibits, it is usually possible to get an overview sense of the whole, which provides a good context for making choices. This is not the case with media, however. Often the extent of the media is hidden, i.e., the length of a video clip, the expectations of the work, the overall nature of what will be presented. Interactive material is notorious for not providing any overview of where a user is going and why he or she might want to go there. Good indexes, maps, and other organizing tools are often missing from museum media.

The Nature of the New Media

Recent developments in technology have provided designers with new tools for introducing media into museum settings. The introduction of new and simple software and hardware tools such as Adobe Photoshop, MacroMedia Director, high-quality scanners, CD-ROM players, video display hardware, and digital video systems, as well as the improvement of consumer and professional video and audio equipment have fostered the increasing integration of computers and computer-generated graphics and text with sounds and images. More and more people are designing and using multimedia systems to provide context to museum exhibits. Many museum exhibitions now include interactive media elements as a matter of course.

To people working in public spaces, new media offers a set of exciting tools to augment their 3-D displays with contextual material, and a way to expand the visitor experience. Through access to rich, interactive kiosks in museums, for example, visitors can move from a glancing experience to a deeper involvement with an underlying idea. And the Internet enables exhibit designers to extend the public experience with content from outside of the museum.

Museum exhibit designers have been quick to take advantage of the fact that multimedia programs are now available for personal computers. Systems now can support a *group experience*— activities where a number of people can interact with one program. The experience also can be *multimodal*, providing a mixture of real images, dynamic models, rich sounds, and tactile sensations. Finally, the media information and experience can be segmented under the control of the user. A piece of video can be viewed, reviewed, stored, and then retrieved for a new purpose.

What is the nature of interactivity? Cybernetics, the study of communication systems and their interactions, has already been applied to public spaces by museum staff, who must anticipate how patrons will move through an exhibit. Just as hands "mouse around" on a computer, in a museum "the feet do the browsing." The layout of information is determined by the space. Interaction with information is not controlled as in film or narrative storytelling; people ask what they want and go where they want. Multimedia design must accommodate the fact that a computer is not just a box; it is responsive, it has a "where-ness." We must devise navigation schemes for traversing information. We are not dealing with just text and graphics; we are constructing multimedia "objects," compositions for use in other situations.

What is the nature of public space? It has staying integrity, yet it is reshaped by use, transformed by participation. The best designs engage people, encourage new experiences, prompt personal actions. We navigate quite naturally through 3-D space. Can we create virtual environments with electronic media and achieve the same coherence of movement and sturdiness of objects as in a physical space? How can we add three-dimensionality to essentially 2-D media?

What is the nature of time? With computers, we expect information on demand; we want a response now. In a public space, we have only brief interactions, even during structured events. How do we negotiate this contrast between "on-demand" versus "ritualized" human experience?

A Framework for Multimedia in Public Space

There are many ways in which media applications fit into public space environments. Sometimes access to a multimedia database provides an important context for an exhibition, or a large-screen interactive video presentation leads to an exciting group experience. The Internet can support remote access to museum exhibits and resources. Different multimedia projects perform different functions, and an individual institution or location may use multimedia in a variety of ways.

It is helps to view these various public space applications in a framework that relates the *nature of the interactivity* to the multimedia system's *relationship to the exhibition*. It is important to understand this relationship because the specific design of a multimedia element and how well it works often depend on the particular setting and its relationship to the whole environment.

There are a variety of ways to use interactive multimedia in public spaces and, in many of them, the nature of the interactivity is quite different. The chart on page 124 presents some of these interrelations.

The horizontal axis describes the nature of the interactivity. For example, one common and important use of interactive media is to support *passive presentation* in an accessible way. Examples

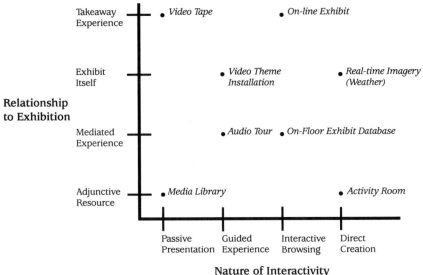

might include a selection of short films on the life and times of a particular artist, or audio programs of railroad sounds associated with an exhibition on steam engines. The hallmark of this type of application is the existence of few choices and somewhat lengthy interactions. Usually, the system is designed to play clips of video or audio, five to 20 minutes in length or maybe longer, that support the context of a particular exhibition or location. Visitors select which clips they want to see at a particular time. Since interactive video and multimedia systems have fewer moving parts than film or videotape machines, they offer greater mechanical reliability. This is an important consideration in a public space setting where the staffing is minimal, and many audio/visual presentations are self-actuated. Since the interaction time is long, the physical comfort of the viewing space is also important.

Guided experiences can be provided by a hand-held audiotape player, interactive CD-audio tour, or a radio handset that receives location-specific stories from a low-power transmitter. With this type of application the visitor can stop the presentation at will and review the material by rewinding the tape or CD-ROM. This type of experience can give visitors a guided tour through an art exhibition or provide atmospheric stories and sounds at a collection of historic ships. The production quality of the material and the personality of the guide (his or her knowledge and authenticity is critical to the success of these applications).

With an *interactive browsing system*, the visitor is able to skim, often quite quickly, through many pieces of information in a database before settling on a particular set of images, text, or sounds. The part of the system one views at any one time may be only a small portion of what is available, and a multimedia database can be outfitted with all sorts of maps, guides, and indices to guide the user. For example, a database of images and background text could support an exhibition of historical objects, or an informational kiosk at a busy downtown location could provide information about the cultural or historical facilities nearby. Here, the framework for navigation becomes an essential tool because of the volume of data available. In this kind of application, the program elements have to be brief and easy to exit, and the interface design has to be very transparent and easy to master, because visitors will allocate only a brief time to it before they move on.

At the far end of this axis are activities where visitors interact directly with the imagery, text, and sounds. They make their choices with the media through *direct creation*, not from a menu or a database navigation system. For example, in a videodisc fly-over of a city, the user controls his own viewing experience; there is little if any mediation between the individual and the material. These multimedia systems allow a people to create their own investigations, their own media projects. A videodisc of a city allows a user to create a tour and to examine in detail a neighborhood of interest. And using a simple computer-based editor, an individual can combine a set of sounds and images related to the objects in a history exhibition and produce a video catalogue to take home for further viewing. The richness of the presentation and the immediacy of the interface is key for these applications.

The vertical axis of the chart represents the physical and/or contextual relationship of the multimedia installation to the exhibition. On one level the interactive media project may serve as an *adjunctive resource* to the exhibition, located typically in an attached library or resource center. Visitors interested in exploring ideas in-depth or dwelling on a particular set of images are able to access additional text and visual material and view it at their own pace at workstations in the center. Separation from the distractions of the primary activity permits longer and more concentrated interactions. For example, a special resource room near to the exhibit floor, outfit-ted with multimedia workstations, activity tables, a stockroom of props, and large projection screens for group viewing, might serve as a lively instruction space for a class on a field trip to a theater muse-um. Staff could present and discuss different versions of plays, and display sets and costumes. And an information kiosk in the lobby could provide information about other cultural events in the city that visitors might find interesting.

Multimedia workstations also can provide information through a *mediated experience* on the exhibit floor itself. Using an interactive multimedia kiosk near a set of displays, a visitor can learn more about the exhibit and answer questions that it may stimulate. For an exhibition on light and color, the workstation might have ani-mated diagrams of the physics of making color as well as many examples of color formation in nature. This type of application sup-ports a fluid back-and-forth relationship between the exhibit and the multimedia system. The visual connections between the exhibit or space and the material in the workstation has to be very strong. And a designer has to pay exceedingly close attention to the physical rela-tionship between the interactive system and the other exhibit ele-ments. All too often the video monitor sticks out like a floating elec-tronic sore thumb, a foreign afterthought among the objects on dis-play.

The multimedia station also may become the primary exhibit itself, where an interactive video provides the main experi-ence. A video showing the slow-motion action of a playground swing or merry-go-round becomes an exhibit on mechanics. A multimedia system provides the visitor with the ability to magnify and analyze an image and compare it to others, or to experiment with light and color in relation to a painter's work. These kinds of presentations are some of the most challenging for designers. It is important to remember that the computer is more than a box with a monitor on top. Large-scale projections, multiple monitors, and dynamic mechanical interfaces to other objects can provide exciting interactions.

Finally, museums can provide the visitor with a *takeaway experience* through the production of a video or audio tape, a videodisc, a CD-ROM, or even remote access to the exhibition through the Internet. Interactive media then becomes an extension of the exhibit itself, and allows visitors to take a piece of their public experience home with them. Videodiscs of city architecture and the collections of a few major art museums already exist. A videodisc and software from a museum might be used by a school group to develop reports after a field trip. Visitors might be able to produce their own multimedia presentations, record them onto videotape at the museum, and take them home. As multimedia platforms become more common, museums will be able to sell take-home experiences that enable visitors to study exhibits in more detail at their leisure.

Conclusion

For all of these applications, the one essential criterion for success is to include the multimedia elements in the overall exhibition or space design right from the start. Too often media seems like an add on, subtracting from the experience rather than enhancing it. The content and the architectural design should drive multimedia development. Media design for public spaces must take its direction from the overall space design if it is to be effective and compelling.

chapter 9

Assuring the Successful Integration of Multimedia Technology in an Art Museum Environment

Scott Sayre

Most museums invest heavily in a variety of strategies to broaden their audience. In order to achieve this, they need to adopt new systems to deliver collection-related information at a variety of levels. These levels of information are often defined according to a person's interest, level of education, age, or the amount of time he has to invest.

Multimedia technology provides a unique vehicle for incorporating different levels of information into an installation and allowing visitors to choose the topics and subject matter best suited to their interests. While novice audiences are accessing contextual information, storytelling, and definitions for basic terminology, sophisticated audiences may be more interested in historical and biographical information, contrasts, comparisons, and bibliographical data. All of this information can be seamlessly integrated into one well-designed multimedia program.

It can be and typically is a very daunting task to integrate any type of technology into a traditional museum environment. Multimedia technology is no exception. This chapter will examine and discuss the opportunities, challenges, and requirements posed by multimedia specific to museums. Issues addressed range from media

Scott Sayre is the director of museum media and technology at the Minneapolis Institute of Arts (MIA). He formed the MIA's Interactive Media Group in early 1991, and since then has led the team in the production of more than eight multimedia programs and the integration of 16 permanent, in-gallery multimedia installations.

justification, development, and evaluation to installation and maintenance. While a number of the issues discussed are specifically pertinent to art museum settings, many have implications for all museums.

Many of the examples and issues covered in this chapter are from a large-scale project at the Minneapolis Institute of Arts (MIA), which in 1990 began to develop and install collection-specific interpretive multimedia programs within a dozen of its major galleries. This project and its collection-by-collection production schedule provides a unique living-laboratory setting to develop, install, and evaluate multimedia programs on an ongoing basis (Sayre 1993).

Justifying a Project: Surveying the Opportunities

Prior to initiating a multimedia project's development, it is often necessary to formally justify the decision to consider multimedia as a viable means of obtaining an institution's goals. Three areas in which multimedia holds unique advantages are in expanding audiences, conveying context, and creating virtual space.

Audience. To a novice visitor, a museum can be a very intimidating place, particularly when it comes to interpretation. Art museums have traditionally catered to visitors who have had some previous experience with art. This audience tends to consist of connoisseurs and people with some education in the arts. Museum didactics and tour information have traditionally been written for visitors possessing some level of previous experience (Eisner, Dobbs 1998). These materials are of limited utility to novice visitors since they rely upon pre-existing knowledge.

Non-traditional and novice audiences appreciate and benefit greatly from additional forms of information beyond standard labels and tours. By making provisions for these new audiences, museums expand the opportunities to capture their interests and begin building their levels of understanding. Multimedia programs can play a pivotal role in attracting these audiences into the most challenging of collection areas and addressing their needs. A 1996 Pew Charitable Trusts-funded visitor study at the Minneapolis Institute of Arts showed that two under-served audiences, African Americans and families, saw the museum's multimedia programs as an attractive way to learn about the MIA and its collections (Herman 1996). Other under-served audiences such as teenagers and men also have been attracted to multimedia as an alternative to traditional didactics.

Context. One of the greatest obstacles museums pose for novice visitors in the interpretation of art is that of context. Tall plaster walls and marble floors that often create a church-like environment may be appropriate for some works but not for others, particularly those from other time periods or cultures. While museums have only been a part of Western culture for a few hundred years, that is not true for many of the works of art within their walls. Ceremonial, religious, and practical objects from daily life are far removed from their original context when placed under glass in little "white" rooms. Some visitors understand the effect of this isolation; others, particularly novice visitors, may not. In some cases visitors may go as far as to assume that the work was created specifically for display in a museum. This assumption may hold true for some contemporary objects, but certainly not historically.

Breaking through contextual barriers can be very difficult within the gallery itself. Once again, the computer holds many unique advantages for expanding the visitor's experience with multimedia-based presentations and simulations. These tools and techniques can be particularly powerful with objects from cultures other than our own. The Minneapolis Institute of Arts has used these tools and techniques for showing the ceremonies in which particular costumes and/or objects are used and placing such items as altarpieces, funerary objects, and furniture into the spaces similar to those they were originally designed to inhabit. After experiencing these departures from the gallery setting, visitors are less prone to be mentally locked within the museum context and more aware of the diversity surrounding them.

Space. Gallery real estate often poses a significant restriction to providing extensive interpretive information for museum visitors. It is almost always a compromise between the number of objects that can be displayed and the amount of space allocated for labels and other interpretive materials. In many cases, didactics lose out to objects, and the visitor's experience is restricted by the limitations of the physical space.

Docent tours, brochures, and audio programs can help to extend the interpretive opportunities. However, the computer holds the advantage of being able to compress a wide range of information within a relatively small space. Well-designed kiosks or in-wall/baffle installations can turn difficult spaces within or adjacent to galleries into information-rich interpretive areas. Ideally, to provide the most effective, seamless integration, these spaces should be considered when a gallery or installation is being designed.

Within the physical space of the installation, the computer creates a vast virtual space. This virtual space is limited primarily by staff time, creativity, hardware, and software, in that order. Beyond these limitations and the financial factors that impact all of them, curators and educators alike can help to create a seemingly endless number of interpretive applications. The MIA has developed virtual interpretive spaces that incorporate such things as a photographic darkroom where visitors can take and print photographs, a Japanese home containing objects from the museum's collection, and ancient art gallery where visitors can tour objects and their "files" in a number of thematic ways. These applications can be expanded or modified over time in response to changing visitor needs or to access additional interpretive resources.

Distributed forms of media such as the World Wide Web can further expand the boundaries of these virtual spaces by creating portholes to dynamic resources developed by other institutions. A 1996 CD-ROM focus group held at the MIA indicated that the expectations many computer users have regarding access to dynamic, comprehensive information has grown immensely with their exposure to the World Wide Web. Knowing that virtually any contemporary computer can access the vast collections of resources available through the Internet makes the thought of accessing just CD-ROM, computer hard disk, or even LAN information seem restricted and frustrating. Web access offers tremendous future reference potential for museum visitors, but also poses daunting, editorial, infrastructure, and support issues for institutions considering opening their galleries to the vast world of external interpretive resources. Network-based projects such as the Art Museum Image Consortium (AMICO) and the Minneapolis Institute of Arts and Walker Art Center's Integrated Art

Information Access (IAIA) project will further encourage museums to provide visitors access to these types of resources.

Development: Making It Happen

Development of museum multimedia programming can be initiated in many different ways depending upon an institution's goals and resources. The decision to produce the programming with internal staff, external freelancers, volunteers, or a commercial development firm can be different for every institution and/or project. While the process of making this decision is a chapter in itself, experience at the MIA has identified a number of issues that always need to be formally addressed, agreed upon, and documented prior to making such decisions and proceeding with any media project. These include:

1. Scope of and commitment to short- and long-term financial support for the project.
2. Definition of primary and secondary audiences.
3. Definition of goals, objectives, and, above all, the scope of the project (including whether it is to be installed internally or distributed externally).
4. Primary interpretive approach(es) and strategies on which the program is based.
5. Identification of the staff member(s) who will be managing the project and the department ultimately responsible for the difficult content-related decisions.
6. Responsibilities and time commitment of internal staff (curators, educators, information systems staff, art/design department, etc.).
7. Importance of the developers' previous experience with the subject matter and approach, the defined audience, and the institution's aesthetic sensibilities.
8. Accessibility and rights to the intellectual assets (audio, images, video, text) to be included in the finished program.
9. Identification of the locations at which the program will be installed and delivered, and the inherent opportunities and restrictions of each.
10. Method for providing ongoing technical support, maintenance, and updating.

Important to all these issues is commitment and consensus of vision. Without such planning and agreement, already expensive and complex media can quickly become a micro-managed, over-budget, off-schedule, out-of-control nightmare. And even with such formal beginnings, many of the costs are hidden in the details and the day-to-day developments. When it comes to multimedia budgets and schedules, the often cited rule is to make your best estimate, then double it. Having a formal plan that includes, but is not limited to, the above issues will help keep the project on course and give everyone something to refer to when things go awry. Chances are, at some point, they will.

Evaluation: Taking Off the Blinders

Evaluation often tends to be an afterthought, or a means for survey-ing the success of a completed project. However, experience at the MIA has shown that thorough evaluation before, during, and after production provides a myriad of benefits in assuring the develop-ment of effective multimedia products. Five different types of tech-niques have been used: pre-production surveys; formative, in-process testing; summative surveys; computer data collection; and, in special cases, audience focus groups.

Pre-production surveys. The objective of these key early surveys is to determine the objects and themes that the target audi-ence is most interested in and identify the areas in which there are unanswered questions. These surveys typically include both observa-tions and interviews and are conducted within the gallery(s) contain-ing the objects. An evaluator (often a volunteer) is located discretely within the galleries and observes and maps out visitor's paths through the rooms, noting the time spent with each object. The eval-uator approaches a predetermined percentage of visitors and asks them whether they have any unanswered questions and to what types of additional information they would like to have access.

Once a significant sample of information has been collect-ed, the findings are summarized into a short document that is dis-tributed to all of the project participants. This is often useful when working with subject-matter experts since it can assist in defining the level at which the target audience is approaching the objects, an excellent starting point for discussing content development.

Formative testing. A program's intuitive qualities determine the ease in which a visitor immediately can start using and understanding it without any prior instructions. This is of particular importance in a museum environment where the multimedia program is meant to be supplemental to the visitor's experience and where a large number of visitors must be served in a short period of time. When developing a program it is very easy to get too committed and too close to an interface and content design without any assurance that it makes sense to the end user. Testing a program with actual visitors during its production reduces assumptions and leads to the creation of a more effective program.

Developers at the MIA often ask visitors using media programs within the museum to spend time with prototype programs. Prototype evaluation is done primarily observing users and conducting short, informal interviews. Even though these evaluations are typically limited by the crudeness of the program itself, they can lead to many helpful findings that often can be incorporated during the remaining stages of design and production.

Summative evaluation. Assessment of a program's successes or failures is often the first thing to be cut when budgets and schedules get tight. However, it is one of the few opportunities to justify formally the investment and to document key issues that can be addressed in revisions or later programs. These types of evaluations can be particularly powerful if designed and used in conjunction with previously conducted pre-production surveys. Together, these instruments can illustrate the effect programs have on visitor dynamics within a gallery or the greater museum.

Similar to the pre-production surveys, the MIA's summative evaluations are conducted through both observations and interviews. Visitors are observed using the program and while browsing in the galleries. A percentage of those visitors are then asked a number of survey questions about the program, its installation, and their experience with related objects in the gallery. The results of the evaluations are compared to the preproduction survey data and then summarized and distributed to the project team. The implications of the findings are discussed in the debriefing meetings following the completion of a project, as well as in pre-production meetings for future projects.

Audience focus groups. Focus groups are appropriate for special situations where a great deal of visitor input is desired. Different from standard forms of assessment, this evaluation technique is designed around an invited group of participants, typically representative of the target audience. Focus groups participate in directed discussions in which all the participants are encouraged to share their feelings and ideas on certain topics and issues, such as those identified in a pre-production visitor survey. Complex topics can be discussed at length, allowing the participants to share opinions and feed off each other's ideas.

Because focus groups often require a significant commitment of time and energy from the participants as well as from the institution, they are often best conducted by an experienced facilitator. The MIA has used audience focus groups for such things as reviewing program topics and design ideas for commercial CD-ROMs.

Computer-collected data. A well-designed program can also serve an important function by evaluating its own activity. During a program's design, counters and time logs can be embedded within the programming to monitor and measure visitor use. Hourly, daily, and weekly statistics can be collected on such things as the popularity of specific sections, sections entered versus sections completed, and average time spent within a section.

The statistical data generated by this type of programming can be correlated with visitor survey data to analyze trends and effects. The MIA collects data from all of its installed programs on a weekly basis. Historical computer data has been used in the study of interface design (Nebenzahl 1993) and in the redesign and modification of existing programs.

Installation: Creating a Home

The physical constraints of the museum environment pose one of the greatest challenges to the integration of multimedia programs. To ensure success, installation issues such as location, physical design, and signage should be decided upon early in the development process. Definition of a program's physical structure and location can serve to formalize and protect the institution's commitment to the program and can also help staff to make interface and content design decisions.

Placement

A commitment of "real estate" to a program formalizes its place in the museum. This decision, while guided by the development team should be an executive decision with full staff agreement. Unless the program is a temporary one, an installation should be thought through and committed to with the same seriousness as any major architectural modification. Ultimately it should become a part of the building's floor plans, aesthetically and technically.

Museums tend to adopt either a centralized or decentralized model of installation. Each model has it's own set of issues, advantages, and disadvantages.

Centralized installations, like those at the National Galleries of Art in Washington, D.C., and London, are designed to function as collections research and reference areas. In these types of installations, multiple terminals accessing the same program are installed within a common, library-like space, located centrally. The program in the installation is comprehensive in nature, spanning the museum's entire collection. Visitors initially can use the program to plan their visit or they can return to the area during the visit to access information on artists, works, and collection areas they found of particular interest.

The primary advantage of centralized installations is that they are within a controlled, staffed physical environment specifically designed for computer use and isolated from the works of art. Visitors can find all of the available computer-based information within one area so there is no confusion about which program they should use. Shared resources such as support staff and printers can be accessed easily by all of the visitors. Visitor traffic can easily be managed through both the floor plan and staff. In addition, because these programs are designed to function in isolation, they do not depend on the existence of the actual objects, and can therefore be more easily reused in a commercially distributed CD-ROM.

The major disadvantage of these types of centralized installations is the way their isolation diverts the visitor's attention away from the actual collection and toward screen reproductions of the objects. This characteristic, in combination with the actual physical isolation, can compromise the continuity of a visitor's learning experience. When touring the galleries, visitors must physically or mentally note the object(s) for which they would like to access further information so they may later research the object(s) when they visit the computer area. A similar situation occurs if the visitors start their visit with the program and then have to carry the information with them into the galleries. In both cases, the visitor's learning experience is broken. And even with computer printouts and maps, visitors are forced to anticipate the objects or information they will find most interesting during their tour of the galleries.

Decentralized installations may take a variety of forms, ranging from freestanding kiosks to gallery-specific media rooms. Art museums integrating decentralized multimedia installations include the San Francisco Museum of Modern Art, the Seattle Museum of Art, and the Minneapolis Institute of Arts. In these institutions, the multimedia programs are installed within or in close proximity to the galleries and are often available in a number of different areas of the museum. Content may be either gallery-specific or general in nature.

One of the advantages of decentralized multimedia installations is the opportunity to integrate them throughout the museum, making them available within the in-gallery experience. Programs can be located in close proximity to the objects to which they relate. In such situations, programs can be designed to interface well with the aesthetics of the specific gallery and/or the surrounding works of art. Most important, programs can make the objects themselves more central to the visitor's experience by directing the viewer's attention to the displays in the gallery.

The disadvantage of decentralized installations is the challenge of the installations themselves. Creating seamless integrations pose many aesthetic as well as technical design challenges, particularly for institutions working within pre-existing gallery and lobby spaces. These spaces must often be redesigned in order to integrate technology as unobtrusively as possible and to assure the best experience possible for all visitors, both program users and non-program users alike. While there are aesthetic and technical design concerns over the computer's enclosure, acoustics, lighting, access, and signage in both centralized and decentralized installations, they are especially critical to the success of the latter.

Design

Successful installation design requires careful consideration of both form and function. And while aesthetic concerns are often first to come to mind in a museum setting, museum visitors and staff typically end up judging an installation's success by its functionality. Determining the type of installation, functional issues such as accessibility, environmental restrictions, and identification can play a significant role in determining the ultimate form the installation will take. Museum installations often take one of three forms: desktop, freestanding, or embedded. Each form has its own set of advantages and disadvantages.

Desktop installations typically have a table or desk that supports the monitor, speakers, and computer. This type of simple design is most suitable for temporary installations where ease of installation and functionality outweighs aesthetic concerns. Since most or all of the equipment is in the open, accessibility poses security and technical problems. Precautions must be taken to insure the safety of the equipment and to restrict vandalism, particularly from technically "inquisitive" children.

Freestanding enclosures, often referred to as kiosks, can offer greater flexibility since they can be designed to serve either seated or standing users and can be easily relocated. Their cabinetry can shroud the equipment, providing a greater level of security and the ability to integrate the design with the aesthetics of the surrounding environment. In some installations, the cabinetry can be designed to match existing casework for an almost seamless integration. In other environments, particularly traditional galleries with high ceilings, kiosk installation is more challenging. Its presence can seem alien, out of place with its surroundings. This often defeats the program's long-term success by making even a "permanent" installation feel temporary. This and the kiosk's "mobility" can significantly reduce an installation's life.

Embedded installations require the greatest up-front financial and design investment. However, the advantages of these enclosures can far outweigh the costs, particularly for long-term or permanent installations. Embedded installations differ from desktop and freestanding installations in that they are, or appear to be, built into the architecture of the building itself. Typically installed in walls or baffles, the equipment supporting these programs is both secure and non-intrusive. The only visible component is the monitor, which is installed to be flush with an existing wall, preserving the sight lines and spatial qualities of the gallery. Embedded enclosures can be designed for either seated or standing audiences. Installations with seats often include a small counter or desk top that extends from the wall, for note taking or supporting items (hands, purses, etc.).

The MIA has found embedded enclosures to be the most successful of all installations, both within the galleries and in separate media spaces. Their high degree of integration with the museum's architecture gives a greater sense of permanence and formally establishes the museum's commitment to multimedia as a form of interpretation.

Logistical and Technical Issues: Making It Work

The success of all forms of installation requires that a great deal of attention is paid to technical and logistical design issues. These issues affect both visitors and museum staff, and include such things as signage, visitor accessibility, lighting and sound control, equipment access, and environmental controls.

Signage. Signs are critical for the visitor's identification and appropriate use of a program. While a single program has the potential of storing a tremendous amount of information, from a distance a glowing screen tells very little about the program itself or the object to which it relates. Directional signage and program identifiers play a key role in attracting visitors and defining the scope of the program. Supporting didactic panels containing such things as timelines and maps can help to set the stage for the program. In some cases, individual object labels can be designed to contain references to the multimedia program containing additional information on the object.

Visitor accessibility. Museum multimedia programs should be as physically and technically accessible as possible. The Americans with Disabilities Act provides an excellent set of standards that must be used to assure that an installation is physically accessible and addresses such important considerations as monitor height and the mobility of surrounding seating. The program's interface and input device(s) must also be designed to be visitor-friendly and intuitive. Intuitive interface designs requiring little or no instruction are the most efficient and least intimidating for non-computer-literate visitors who want to access information quickly. Simple input devices such as touch screens also tend to be more user friendly for visitors unfamiliar with screen-independent input devices, such as trackballs, joy sticks, and mice.

Lighting control. Uncontrolled direct and reflected room light can significantly affect the visual quality of a multimedia program. Steps should be taken during the installation design to reduce or eliminate light falling directly on the computer's screen, which can drastically effect the screen's readability and reproduction of color. Care also needs to be taken to position the screen so that it does not reflect the light of surrounding objects or surfaces. Flat-screen monitors are the least susceptible to reflection and read better than monitors with anti-reflection coatings, which tend to reduce overall image quality.

Sound control. The audio produced by a multimedia program can affect both the program's users and the surrounding visitors. Headphones may be a solution in some cases; however, issues of hygiene, maintenance, and multiple viewers restrict their usefulness. Although challenging, amplified speakers can be used in most museum environments if acoustical design and speaker placement is considered at the beginning of an installation's design. Careful attention needs to be paid to a speaker's pattern (the direction in which it naturally projects sound), its placement, its proximity to the user's ears, and the placement of acoustically absorbent and reflective surfaces.

Equipment access. Hardware and software adjustment and maintenance requires that support staff have easy access to all of the computer equipment. This can be particularly challenging with kiosks and embedded installations, where the equipment is secured in some type of cabinetry. Ease of access for preventative maintenance and repair helps to reduce program downtime. Efficient designs allow work to be done on a program while it is installed and facilitate easy removal and replacement of equipment. Many of the MIA's installation designs incorporate removable equipment carts, which allow all of the equipment to be removed, switched, or installed as one mobile component.

Environmental controls. Museum environments can be very hard on delicate computer hardware unless the proper precautions are taken to reduce a component's exposure to excessive dust and heat. Enclosures for permanent installations should be designed to seal tightly around the equipment. Concurrently, precautions should be taken to ensure that the sealed space is adequately cooled and ventilated to prevent overheating of the equipment. This can be easily remedied with the installation of vents with replaceable filters at the bottom of the cabinet and adequate cooling fans, to extract heated air, at the top.

Maintenance and Support: Keeping It Up

Significant steps should be taken to assure that multimedia installations are never "out of order." However, once installed, every public multimedia program requires some degree of on-going updating, maintenance, and support. Well-designed programs and installations can significantly reduce these demands. And the best-laid plans will include budgets for ongoing maintenance and equipment upkeep.

Updating. The amount of updating a software program needs is dependent on its design and the institution's ongoing commitment to it. Encyclopedic programs and those addressing living artists may need to be updated each time there is a new acquisition or a change in an artist's life. In other cases, unanticipated design problems or a change in the surrounding gallery aesthetics may require small changes to a program's design or content in order to make it effective for users.

Preventative maintenance. Regularly scheduled maintenance is key to keeping a program looking and working well. Most of this type maintenance is directed at keeping the equipment and installation clean. Monitors and other exposed surfaces should be cleaned on a daily basis to keep the program looking new and freshly installed. Just a few fingerprints on a computer screen can drastically reduce a program's overall visual quality and attractiveness to the visitor. More extensive cleanings of the equipment and cabinet interior(s) should be conducted on a monthly to quarterly basis, depending upon the air quality of the installation environment. These extensive cleanings require the removal and cleaning of all of the internal equipment. This is necessary to combat the progressive build up of dust and dirt electronic equipment naturally attracts. During this cleaning, all equipment should be opened and blown with compressed air and the cabinet vacuumed and wiped clean. Filter materials also should be cleaned and replaced regular basis. These preventative steps significantly reduce heat buildup and extend the equipment's working life.

Equipment life. Even with the best preventative maintenance, publicly installed computer equipment has a limited operating life. Budgets for long-term multimedia installations should include the costs of equipment repair and replacement. Large-screen computer monitors tend to be the components that require the most attention and have the shortest functional life-span.

While monitors will operate as long as most other computer equipment, their characteristics, such as contrast and color balance, shift dramatically over time. Hardware and software adjustments will only compensate for this shifting during the first two to three years of a monitor's installed life. Eventually, the constant operation permanently affects the screen's phosphors to a point where they can no longer be corrected. Experiences at the MIA have shown it to be more cost-effective to replace monitors at this point than to attempt to have them repaired. Computers are also prone to component failure after years of operation. In most cases, these components can easily be repaired or replaced. Interestingly enough, the most common reason for computer replacement results from changing visitor expectations in computer speed and responsiveness.

Future Issues and Opportunities

If anything is definite about museum media installations, it is that they are constantly evolving and continue to provide developers with new challenges and capabilities. And as the technologies continue to evolve, so do user expectations. The increasing prevalence of networked media in people's day-to-day lives continues to expand the visitor's thirst for information. Since museums cannot afford to continuously ride on the cutting edge of technology, they must be selective in their investments. No matter how tempting the emerging technologies may be, the primary criteria for making investment and design decisions should always be determined by the technologies' ability to achieve a discrete set of formally defined objectives. With this goal in mind, any institution can continue to move ahead with a greater degree of confidence.

References

Eisner, E., and S. Dobbs. 1988. Silent pedagogy: How museums help visitors experience exhibitions. *Art Education* 41, no. 4: 6-15.

Herman, D. 1996. Minneapolis Institute of Arts: Pew visitor evaluation. Minneapolis: Minneapolis Institute of Arts.

Nebenzahl, L. 1993. Evaluating interface design through user data collection. In *Museums and interactive multimedia: Proceedings of the sixth international conference of the MDA and the second international conference on hypermedia and interactivity in museums.* Edited by Diane Lees. Cambridge, England: Museum Documentation Association Archives and Museum Informatics, pp. 198-203.

Sayre, S. 1993. The evolution of interactive interpretive media: A report on discovery and progress at the Minneapolis Institute of Arts. In *Museums and interactive multimedia: Proceedings of the sixth international conference of the MDA and the second international conference on hypermedia and interactivity in museums.* Edited by Diane Lees. Cambridge, England: Museum Documentation Association Archives and Museum Informatics, pp. 41-51.

chapter 10

A Place for the Muses? Negotiating the Role of Technology in Museums

Kristine Morrissey and Douglas Worts

Neil Postman, the noted educator, has suggested that museums represent an attempt to answer the fundamental question "What does it mean to be human?" As individuals, we try to make sense of our lives by exploring the relationships between what we think and do, and the rest of our natural and cultural environment. Objects are a link to this larger context of time and place, between personal experiences and that of the human experience. Objects can symbolize, recall, or illuminate something that has meaning to us—a relationship, a place, an accomplishment, a time. As individuals, we collect objects that connect us to other people, places, and times. As institutions, museums collect objects for the same reasons, as they try to document collective standards of quality and provide insights into cultural trends. At the end of the 1990s, museums are facing questions that challenge their identity and purpose, largely because our increasingly "multicultural" and technological society has become more complex, which has led to new relationships among people, objects, and museums.

As our cultures attempt to redefine what it means to be a family, a community, a school, a political party, and even a nation, is it any wonder that museums—dedicated to reflecting, preserving,

Kristine Morrissey is curator of interpretation at the Michigan State University Museum in East Lansing, and teaches museum education and educational technology courses at Michigan State University. Douglas Worts is an educator/evaluator in the Canadian art department at the Art Gallery of Ontario, Toronto, Canada. He teaches a graduate course in museum education within the museum studies program at the University of Toronto.

defining, and influencing culture—find it difficult to establish their place, and struggle to know what to reflect or preserve? The dilemma of identity and the even more fundamental question of who should define this identity are not new. In the past, changes in society, public opinion, politics, or economics have periodically challenged museums to reconsider issues of authenticity, power, control, access, representation, and empowerment of both individuals and groups. But the discussion is different today in part because of technology. Advances in technology are changing society's processes and products; they are transforming our understanding of where information originates, how it is disseminated and used, who owns it, and where and how it resides. Technology is also revolutionizing how we communicate and relate with one another.

If museums don't have a clear understanding of their relationships with information, communication, and their public, they not only miss the opportunity to effectively utilize technology's power to help transform these relationships, but run the greater risk of losing sight and control of what they become. In the book, *The Future Does Not Compute*, Stephen Talbott discusses the power of technology to shape our lives if we are not fully conscious of and responsible about how we use it. He reminds us that "what we have made, makes us" (Talbott 1995, p. 6).

Discussions of technology must start with who we are and who we want to be as museums and as museum professionals within the context of our disciplines, communities, cultures, and countries. Issues of control, empowerment, representation, authenticity, and scholarship must all be reconsidered within the context of the power and the seductiveness of technology. This chapter discusses some of the fundamental issues of museum identity and then explores implications for the development of technology-based operations.

Creating a Place for the Muses

Three experiences of the muses in museums:

A child gazes at the skull of an African elephant. After a nod from his parent, he reaches out to touch the tusk, his face showing the thrill of contact with such a creature. An older

Experiencing the muses in a museum: A child gazes at the skull of an elephant, while another touches a dinosaur fossil. Photos by Kristine Morrissey and Timothy Trumble.

man calls his son's attention to various parts of an exhibit on Mexican celebrations, animatedly sharing memories of his home country. A woman looks at a painting of a beaver dam in the Canadian northland while listening to an audio recording, and enters the world of her imagination as memories, feelings, images, and associations flood her mind.

The nine muses of Greek mythology were the daughters of Zeus and Mnemosyme, the goddess of memory. They were sources of inspiration in the arts and sciences and, according to Greek and Roman mythology, a person inspired by the muses was more sacred than a priest. Museums have been viewed as "temples of the muses" that provide humanity with sources of inspiration and function as the keepers of memories. In the age of digital communication and virtual realities, are museums still "temples of the muses"? Are they sources of inspiration and awe, keepers of memories? Or are they, like the immortal gods were to many in their time, interesting but essentially irrelevant to the activities of daily life? What is the relationship among museums, people, objects, and memory? What role does and should technology play in this relationship?

In the early 1970s, Duncan Cameron, then director of the Brooklyn Museum, wrote a think-piece on the role of museums entitled "The Museum: A Temple or the Forum." The concepts of *temple* and *forum* provide a useful construct for considering the dilemma of creating institutions that can both foster timely social meanings in the age of information and serve as sacred places where the muses offer insight and inspiration.

A *temple* implies a sacred space, involving not simply encounters with selected objects, but with the muses—which can be considered creative, symbolic experiences with aspects of the human psyche, both personal and collective. Psychologically, interaction with the muses can be thought of as interactions between a conscious ego and one's unconscious, leading to new awareness. These symbolic experiences are usually associated with insight, mystery, awe, and strong emotions, as well as a feeling of connection to a past and a position within the present. What then is the role of the temple in such an experience? A temple is a special, physical place that helps individuals to create a connection between the conscious and the unconscious. Temples often contain objects that are thought to have special symbolic status, linking the present with a spiritual realm. Often, mystery, authority, and rituals are combined with regular contact in order to facilitate the "temple experience." There is little doubt that a museum has some of the attributes of a temple— special objects, imposing architecture that creates an out-of-the-ordinary environment, and a mysterious power that inhabits the space. But whether museums are capable of truly functioning as temples is a question that needs to be addressed.

Like the temple, a *forum* is both a physical and a psychological space. Ideally, it is a place where ideas, daily activities, memories, dreams, joys, fears, and questions can be shared, positions can be argued, and issues can be considered. It is a place where individuals come together to share the task of understanding our present and defining our future as individuals, as groups, and as cultures. But a forum is a complex environment to create. It has to be neutral in order to enable conversation and to transcend unfair power struggles. There must be wisdom in the management of the interactions. And there has to be respect amongst the participants for all parties involved. These conditions are not easy to achieve.

Cameron argued that museums needed to play both roles, but that this could not happen simultaneously. It is questionable whether museums have ever managed either to become the sacred spaces of temples or harness the dynamic processes of true forums. Nonetheless, if museums were committed to realizing both the concept of sacred space and that of forum, then many of the cultural and social needs of our society could be better addressed. Only in understanding, accepting, and balancing both these functions can museums find their place in this challenging age of technology.

If museums are to perform some of the functions of temples, they need to carefully consider the role of physical space, the types of experiences that characterize an experience of the sacred, the symbolic role of objects, and the critical role of communication. Physical spaces reach their full potential as sacred spaces only when they exist in relationship to the sacred space within the individual who visits. If the temple reflects the collective beliefs, history, accomplishments, and sufferings of a group within society, it is essential that individuals who come there experience their own personal and authentic manifestations of those stories, feelings, and images.

While museums have long been accepted as being important to any modern society, charges of irrelevance or elitism mirror increasing social and political pressures for greater equality in representation and equal access to power for individuals in all spheres of our daily lives. The concept of a forum suggests that museums can extend beyond the authoritative roles of traditional museums to serve as a context where individual and group knowledge and experiences are shared, interpreted, and passed on, thus becoming part of the living and evolving dimension of culture. A forum is based on a process of shared dialogue that accepts and integrates the authenticity of the knowledge and experiences of all visitors, museum professionals, and communities.

In today's society, there are fewer opportunities to discuss community, family, or personal histories and lore, or even the events of the day. Museum objects and exhibits can help to fill this need, by evoking memories and stimulating plans, questions, or thoughts about daily activities. A mounted bear reminds a child of the book he read in school; an exhibit on mourning rituals stimulates discussions among visitors and museum staff about memories of lost ones and philosophical and religious issues. These types of encounters facilitate a process of self-expression and affirmation. Within social groups, each person not only experiences the exhibit differently, but experiences the relationships within the group differently.

With few exceptions, museums have only recently begun to truly embrace the function of the forum and are finding it difficult to balance this effort with the history and responsibilities associated with scholarship and traditional practice. To truly embrace the concept of the forum, museums need to address issues of trust, empowerment, and representation. Individuals must feel that their experiences and opinions are welcome and appropriate. They must feel that the museum is committed to the idea of a forum and to a process of fair and considered reflection.

In the information age, the source of meaning for museums will lie in their ability to put themselves in the center of the individual's search for connections, to become a forum for society to address the questions of meaning, to create an environment where the knowledge and assumptions about our environment and our culture are explored and continually re-created, not just by museum professionals, but by all interested members of the public. This requires a thoughtful examination of how insight comes to individuals, how they find and create meaning, and how interaction between individuals and objects sparks insight and feelings of connection. It requires changing our perspective from disseminating information to facilitating the search for knowledge.

Beyond Information

Truly speaking, it is not instruction but provocation that I can receive from another soul.
—Ralph Waldo Emerson
quoted in Interpreting Our Heritage

Today we create and disseminate information faster than at any time in our history. But are we any better at synthesizing, analyzing, evaluating, and applying information? Do we know how to use this information to improve ourselves, our families, communities, churches, schools, and other institutions? If museums consider themselves in the business of creating, finding, and disseminating "information," it is easy to move to the next step of using technology to help us provide *more* information to more people. Today's technology can provide visitors with information not just through exhibitions, labels, catalogues, and other traditional interpretive methods, but through CD-ROMs, extensive databases, virtual museums, World Wide Web sites, and a variety of other formats. Although the new interfaces are exciting, the relationship between the data and the visitor is not necessarily or fundamentally changed simply because the amount of data and choices has increased.

Too much information creates what Richard Saul Wurman, author of *Information Anxiety*, describes as the black hole between data and knowledge. Wurman quotes from Michael Crichton's book, *Electronic Life: How to Think About Computers*: "It's disquieting to hear that computers will provide us with more information . . . what people really intend when they speak of information is meaning, not facts" (Wurman 1989, p. 36). Indeed, decades of research have shown that visitors are often overwhelmed by the amount of information in museums and have difficulty relating it to themselves. Many critics of the current emphasis on wholesale adoption of technology suggest that it is threatening our culture, seducing and intimidating us with overwhelming amounts of disconnected and discontinuous data at the cost of our search for knowledge.

Museums are meaningful not when they simply provide information but when they help visitors make sense of that information. They are meaningful when individuals or groups can examine their own experiences and thoughts in a larger or different context. Freeman Tilden, the great advocate of interpretation and author of the historically popular book *Interpreting Our Heritage*, describes interpretation as "an educational activity which aims to reveal meanings and relationships . . . rather than simply to communicate factual information," or more simply as "revelation based upon information" (Tilden 1957, p. 8).

In the article "Visitor Meaning-Making in Museums for a New Age," Lois Silverman suggests that the meanings and strategies visitors construct appear to cluster around "two broad and pervasive human needs: the need for *individuality*, including uniqueness and autonomy; and the need for *community*, including affiliation and interdependence" (Silverman 1995, p. 164). As museums increasingly encourage visitors to join in a dialogue about the ongoing construction of meaning around cultural and natural objects, the tensions between scholarship and other forms of meaning-making become more acute.

It is true that museum scholars, representing various academic fields, contribute to the growth of knowledge within society. They have specialized training, expertise, knowledge, and a commitment that have led them into a complex relationship with objects and knowledge through field work, collecting, research, interpretation, or some other types of interaction with objects. Their responsibility to a discipline and the value of their knowledge and commitment cannot be minimized in this time of change. However, this needs to be balanced and integrated with the recognition that there are many ways to see, study, and express history, culture, and science. This recognition leads naturally to a view of communication as a process of dialogue, rather than monologue—in turn part of a commitment to a relationship with the public.

Museums as Dialogue

The life channel of the information age is communication.
—John Naisbitt

Museums have been challenged on many fronts to recognize that the stories they have traditionally told and the cultures they have most often represented have not been inclusive or dynamic. This comes at a time of rapid change in the demographic political structures of our societies. The repatriation of certain objects to Native American groups, the continued reactions to the viewpoint of some exhibits (such as the *Enola Gay* exhibit), as well as the growth and popularity of museums representing the perspectives or experiences of cultural groups (such as the United States Holocaust Memorial Museum, National Museum of Women in the Arts, and Native American museums) and the emergence of children's museums, all speak to the growing interest in changing not only the content but the perspective of the museum—acknowledging that *who* tells the story is a critical part of the story. Of the 10 *Excellence and Equity* principles put forth by the American Association of Museums, at least five refer to the need for more collaboration or acknowledgment of diversity. The fifth principle calls on museums to "assure that the interpretive process manifests a variety in cultural and intellectual perspectives and reflects an appreciation for the diversity of the museums' public."

A more inclusive approach to public programming in museums will affect all aspects of museum operations, from the ways technology is used to how research is approached to strategies for collecting, exhibiting, and interpreting. The approach will have to go beyond including stories *about* women, children, or the working class to changing the questions we ask and the ways we investigate and react to science, history, culture, and art. In the book *Gender Perspectives*, Edith P. Mayo's essay discusses how critical the perspective is in approaching history. She states: "Not until the theories and methodologies by which we research, write and understand history are defined by women as well as by men; not until the constructions by which history is created and written become angles of vision held by women and not by men; not until the questions we ask of history are defined also by women . . . will we see meaningful women's history in museums" (Glaser and Zenetou 1994, p. 61).

Although all perspectives can never be represented, technology offers great promise in providing and collecting multiple perspectives and can provide a forum for museums to acknowledge and discuss the natural biases that frame their handling of an issue. This shift toward more inclusive interpretive approaches also affects the dynamics and communication patterns among museum staff. It painfully challenges the traditional boundaries generally defined by training or position such as educator, curator, marketing professional, or director.

Used thoughtfully, technology can help us begin and maintain authentic dialogue among museums professionals, visitors, and the public. It can facilitate a change in the dynamics between museums and visitors as we recognize that we are partners in what museums are ultimately about—exploring and expressing our piece of the human experience.

A Starting Place for Using Technology

All of the things I have done with technology first involved wondering what is actually going on in the person and then wondering what the technology could do to amplify it. . . .

—Alan Kay
quoted in The Art of Human-Computer Interface Design

In *The Museum Experience*, Falk and Dierking suggest that the exhibit design process should begin by "thinking about how the visitor might use the knowledge presented in the exhibits rather than thinking about what objects to exhibit or what ideas to present" (Falk and

Dierking 1992, p. 142). This reflects the shift in museums away from the traditional authoritarian paradigm of interpretation toward a relationship based on mutual respect and shared goals. In the book *Planning for People in Museum Exhibitions*, Kathleen McLean encourages museums to consider visitors as partners in the exhibit design process (McLean 1993).

If we start our discussions of technology with what is happening in the visitor's mind and how experiences with technology can amplify that, our questions change. Instead of asking "How can I use computers or multimedia in this exhibit?" or "How can I show off our collections, our research?," we ask, "How will visitors relate to this object? What type of interaction will illuminate or enhance the relationship between visitors and this object? How will they experience the exhibit, the museum, or their environment differently after this interaction?"

This leads us away from thinking about interactions with computers or the World Wide Web to considering interaction with ideas, thoughts, objects, questions, and each other. We begin to think about *processes* rather than just *content*. What types of activities will address the needs for individuality and community? How can technology help visitors reflect, reminisce, imagine, evaluate, compare, analyze, create, and express?

It has often been said that it is difficult to evaluate technology. Those evaluations that are conducted often look most closely at the relationship between the visitor and the technology rather than at the interaction between the visitor and the museum and how technology influences that relationship. Evaluation should start before development of any interpretive approach (including media and technology), assessing visitor attitudes and their relationship with the content or the exhibit and with interest levels. After development, we need to focus on the relationship between the visitor and the content or exhibits as well as the relationship between the visitor and the technology and how this interaction fits within the mission of the institution.

The next section of this discussion is organized around strategies for using technologies. Technology is considered broadly as any type of electronic communication tool including audio, video, computers, networks, and virtual realities, among others. The strategies are by no means a definitive list but represent a variety of formats, types of museums, and budgets and activities that provide interpretation and provocation, promote dialogue and creative meaning-making, and integrate scholarship with meaning-making. They are based on the belief that visitors should leave a museum experience (whether it is inside or outside the institution's walls) feeling more engaged, thoughtful, in-touch, and responsible and with a better sense of who they are and how they are connected to and contribute to their culture and their natural environment.

Interpretive Strategies for Using Technology

Visitor-centered interpretive strategies personalize and contextualize the museum experience. Personalizing relates the content or the programs of the museum to the identity (past experiences, attitudes, values, fears, etc.) of the visitor. It helps individuals realize their potential to think, feel, do, imagine, relate. Contextualizing helps visitors understand or reflect on their experiences within shared value, belief, and knowledge systems.

Examples of interpretive strategies:
1. Bring the visitor's story into the interpretive process.
2. Involve the public not just as consumers, but as creators and contributors.
3. Connect the content to the activities of the visitor's life.
4. Connect objects to people, places, purpose.
5. Connect people to people.
6. Connect people to resources.
7. Facilitate and encourage playfulness.
8. Personalize the message through stories and narrative.
9. Involve visitors in making decisions, choices, judgments.
10. Provide multiple perspectives or viewpoints.
11. Create responsive environments.
12. Provide relevant information.

Strategy: Bring the visitor's story and experience into the interpretation.

Visitors are a rich resource that is often untapped in the interpretation of an exhibit or program. They bring to the museum their past experiences, knowledge, curiosity, memories, and their unique way of thinking about objects. Unfortunately, museums often follow the motto of "Leave nothing but footprints, take nothing but photographs." Technology can provide a mechanism for visitors to leave behind a piece of themselves, thereby not only engaging in self-expression and affirmation, but adding to the richness of the story the next visitor will experience. This may take the form of an inter-active comment or question book, a database where visitors add their memories and writings, or a multimedia program that captures images or words of visitors and integrates them into an existing data-base, Web page, or other format.

Strategy: Involve visitors not just as consumers but as creators and contributors.

Knowledge is reinforced when it is expressed and shared. Technology-based programs can encourage visitors to respond to exhibits and ideas through the creation of art, writing, image manip-ulations, or take-home, visitor-designed exhibits, catalogues, or museum tours. Many museums have begun using technology in this way, particularly with young visitors who are sometimes not ade-quately engaged or challenged by traditional passive presentations in museums.

In CitySpace, part of the Exploratorium's 4,000-square-foot MultiMedia Playground '95, kids designed buildings using personal computers and then placed them within a growing city. Kid's Express, a program at the Indianapolis Children's Museum, involves teenagers in all aspects of newspaper production, including research, writing, image preparation, page layout, and printing. The project uses tech-nology in a way that both encourages students' efforts and perspec-tives and provides a product for the public.

Strategy: Connect the content of the exhibit to the activities of the visitor's life.

Museums often deal with abstract concepts and principles. Even when visitors feel that an exhibit tells an important story, they don't necessarily feel connected to it or that they are a part of it. In discussing the role of intrinsic motivation, Mihály Csikszentmihályi and Kim Hermanson write, "Most important, the link between the museum and the visitor's life needs to be made clear." Technology can engage visitors in activities that help them apply what they know to the content of the exhibit or, conversely, apply the content of the exhibit to their daily activities and decisions (Csikszentmihályi and Hermanson 1995, p. 35).

An example is the "Home Water Audit" developed by the New Mexico Museum of Natural History and Science as part of a temporary exhibit called "Arid Lands, Sacred Waters." The message of the exhibit—that water is a precious and scarce resource—became less abstract and more personal through this simple hypercard program in which users learned the consequences of their daily activities. After answering questions such as "Do you adjust the water size when you wash clothes?," users learn how much water they use daily and how much they can save through alternative behaviors such as adjusting water for the size of a laundry load.

Strategy: Connect objects to people, places, purpose.

Much of the meaning of objects resides in their physical, historical, and sociological context. Technology cannot reproduce this context, but it can create a link between objects and people, places, or purposes. One particularly effective strategy is to integrate the voice and the perspective of the person(s) who created, used, collected, or found the object.

In the exhibit "Ethiopia: Traditions of Creativity" at the Michigan State University Museum, 11 video vignettes show the Ethiopians who created the objects displayed in the exhibit. A weaver and his son work outside on a handmade loom, a Harari basketmaker is shown in her home below a display of her baskets, and a contemporary painter discusses his art and the identity of Ethiopian culture. Viewers felt that they learned about the objects in a uniquely personal way and felt more appreciation of the creativity involved because they could connect the objects to a process, an individual, and a culture. One visitor said, "It was like learning about the culture but learning through people. . . ." Another visitor with two young children said, "It seemed real to me versus when you go to a traditional museum" (interview with Michigan State University graduate student Margaret Ropp).

Technology effectively engages visitors when it becomes

invisible and the user can interact with another person. After using a multimedia program called "Making Sense of Modern Art" at the San Francisco Museum of Modern Art, a visitor commented that "the computer just disappears. . . . I was just focusing on, like, having a conversation with Dorothea Lange or listening to her" (interview with Peter Samis, program manager at the San Francisco Museum of Modern Art). The program he was using integrates photographs and video and audio segments with reflections by artists, art historians, and critics. The visitor went on to say that ". . . museums can be very, very off-putting places. I'm sensitive of always being . . . working in . . . the sort of sanctification of art and of literature that happens. And I think that this, the accessibility of this, and its, sort of its humanness, the interactive aspect of it changes the nature of the museum."

Strategy: Connect people to people.

Technology can create forums for dialogue between and among people in different sites, across disciplines and ages, and without the limitations of time or location. Perhaps the most obvious examples are the popularity of World Wide Web pages, Internet addresses, and electronic bulletin boards. The popularity and relevance of these lists are evident in the number and increased specificity of topic and audience. The Museum–L discussion list had over 1,700 subscribers in 1997 after starting with less than 20 people in 1991. H-Net has more than 70 lists with about 40,000 subscribers, including humanities scholars, professors, students, and others interested in the humanities.

As technology quickly becomes a popular interface between museums and the public, we need to consider whether changing the arena of our communication changes its nature. Does it influence the subjects we talk about or avoid? Will this type of communication compete with face-to-face interaction, or lull us into a complacent belief that they are the same? If we spend an afternoon talking with dozens of colleagues on the Internet but don't stray into our galleries to talk with visitors and other staff, what have we traded?

Just as the highways and jets that promised to connect parts of the world also led to commuter marriages, children growing up distant from their cousins, and neighbors that change regularly, we cannot assume that the wonderful resource of increased access to people via electronic networks won't also have a price. We need to monitor our electronic communications and make sure they continue to connect and not separate us from our public. We must continually assess whether communication is two-way and inclusive.

Strategy: Connect people to resources.

Just as the format of technology shapes communication, it also affects the definition and characteristics of the audience served, the nature of the interaction, and the type of resource offered. Museums are now using the capabilities of electronic connections to provide access to their traditional resources (images of objects, information about programs and hours, etc.), as well as offering new types of resources and reaching new audiences.

The Science Learning Network collaboration was created to offer on-line demonstration schools, an on-line electronic librarian, professional development in telecomputing for science educators, and other resources to support teaching and learning in science. The Smithsonian offered a Web-based interactive version of the exhibit "Ocean Planet" along with curriculum materials, a message board, ideas for hands-on projects, and links to other related sites including aquariums (see chapter 11). The Library of Congress's "American Memory" project provides digitized versions of original source documents. Offering documents written in a historical figure's own hand, historical moving pictures, photographs, and sound recordings to classrooms and homes, it creates a different environment and attitude toward learning history.

As museums turn their attention and resources to going on-line, we must remember that not all schools, classrooms, and homes have equal access to technology. In this era of limited resources, we must consider the needs of users before we succumb to the seduction of the new technologies and abandon more traditional methods of delivery such as videotapes or print materials.

Strategy: Use technology to facilitate play.

What are human beings meant to do? In his book *Virtual Reality*, Howard Rheingold proposes that the answer is "play." He suggests that play is seen an as antonym to "work," whereas actually, it is "our most important thinking tool" and closely related to the processes involved in science, art, and all the disciplines that require us to learn to think in new ways. He cites Bruno Bettleheim's use of the German term *spielraum*, meaning plenty of room "to move not only one's elbows but also one's mind, to experiment with things and ideas at one's leisure, or to put it colloquially, to toy with ideas" (Rheingold 1991, p. 372).

In museums, play takes on special meaning in an environment where most participants are there by free choice, during leisure time, and often within a social group—at least partially motivated by the urge to share a "nice time." Deborah Perry, a museum evaluator and researcher, has identified six affective variables that describe what museum visitors want: curiosity, confidence, challenge, control, play, and communication. She suggests that play is often underestimated in its ability to facilitate learning by incorporating both imagination and sensory enjoyment (Perry 1994, p. 71). Technology, with its ability to support interaction and multiple media formats, can provide a forum or a container for creative play where visitors creatively experiment with tools, concepts, relationships, and various aspects of art, history, science, and other ways of looking at experiences.

Strategy: Personalize the message through stories and narrative.

The power of storytelling and narrative continues to capture attention and imagination, providing context, drama, and personal connections. Stories and individual perspectives can evoke an empathetic or sympathetic response that helps visitors personalize the message. In his musings about virtual realities, Rheingold discusses the origins of drama and the importance of catharsis as a healthy and necessary way for people to deal with the themes of life and death. He suggests that an understanding of how we provoke or stimulate catharsis might become a foundation of the emerging psychological investigation of virtual experience.

The Minnesota History Center uses a variety of media formats to bring stories and personal narrative into the interpretive presentation of their exhibits. In an exhibit on communities, visitors sit in the passenger section of a simulated plane and Vietnam War veterans reflect on their feelings during their journey to Vietnam. In the exhibit "Minnesota A to Z," the letter "V," for voices, presents the experiences of real people using audio from a rich oral history collection. As part of an exhibit on families, a multimedia program called "Everything Must Change" integrates actual objects on a stage with a media presentation about the events and rituals that mark important stages of life.

In "A More Perfect Union," an exhibition at the Smithsonian's National Museum of American History about the treatment of Japanese Americans during WWII, a simulation of a Spartan room in a simple wood building includes numerous beds, trunks, a table, and a clothesline. These objects evoke curiosity about how this room was used. Through the use of a continuous-loop, backscreen-projected film, a man and child appear at a doorway. The adult starts telling the child about his experiences living in this room: He and other Japanese Americans were forced into internment camps during WWII. The very real dialogue engages emotional faculties and evokes an empathic connection between visitors and history. Viewers integrate the information into their existing world view, thus encouraging their imaginations to acknowledge the capacity for human cruelty in our society.

Strategy: Engage visitors in making decisions, choices, and evaluations.

Perhaps one of the most common outcomes of a museum visit is not the acquisition of new information, but the opportunity to apply or synthesize existing knowledge. Activities that engage visitors in making choices, decisions, or evaluations are likely to engage their imaginations and intellects and encourage "mindfulness" rather than the "mindlessness" that can overcome museum audiences. Decision-making activities can also encourage social interaction as families or friends discuss alternatives and potential consequences of choices, leading to a deeper level of processing or synthesizing content.

At the end of the "Science in American Life" exhibit at the National Museum of American History, a computer program asks visitors a series of questions regarding their attitudes about science and scientists. Responses are added to a database; a chart displays the distribution of answers. People have an opportunity to compare their attitudes to those of other museum visitors, thereby heightening an awareness not only of their own attitudes but of how they fit within a larger social context.

Strategy: Provide multiple perspectives and viewpoints.

Providing multiple perspectives can balance the picture and assure visitors that there are many ways to understand or interpret events and objects. This can increase their confidence in their own knowledge and interpretive abilities. The viewpoints may represent different disciplines, levels of expertise (an expert versus a novice), relationships with the object (user, collector, creator), theories or philosophical issues ("Is clear-cutting ultimately good for the environment?" or "Are dinosaurs related to birds?"). Technology can also engage visitors in making choices or analyses and reacting to theories.

This approach fosters a richer understanding of the complexity of most issues and encourages visitors to view a discipline (history, science, economics, etc.) as a dynamic process of forming, testing, and evaluating hypotheses rather than as a static body of content.

Strategy: Create responsive environments.

What is the relationship between ambient temperature and the internal temperature of a reptile or of a mammal? How does changing the ambient temperature affect a so-called "cold-blooded" or "warm-blooded" animal? Labels can explain this, and realistic walk-through immersion dioramas can depict a desert scene with reptiles and mammals, but neither allows visitors to see the dynamic relationship between those two temperatures, which is crucial to understanding why it is inaccurate to describe reptiles as "cold-blooded" and mammals as "warm-blooded."

Computer technology can create responsive environments in which visitors manipulate variables and experience the consequences, helping them recognize the relationship between variables. While simulations have been popular for a long time, they are sometimes superficial, and the variables manipulated and the consequences may not approximate the natural world. In the book *Virtual Reality*, Brenda Laurel, who has promoted the concept of technology as theater, envisions dramatically created worlds "where characters make choices with clear causal connections to outcomes, where larger forces like ethics, fate or serendipity form constellations of meaning that are only rarely afforded by the real world. . . . If we can make such worlds interactive, where a user's choices and actions can flow through the dramatic lens, then we will enable an exercise of the imagination, intellect, and spirit that is of an entirely new order" (Rheingold 1991, p. 306). Virtual realities and graphic capabilities will provide unimagined opportunities to create responsive environments, but it is up to us to determine whether we will use the power to pursue authenticity or attractive but superficial "bells and whistles."

Strategy: Provide relevant information.

There is clearly a role for technology as a provider of information. Overviews or orientations allow visitors to print out their own floor plans of museums or quickly find a specific exhibit or information about daily programs. A Web site can provide information for teachers; a photo CD can provide images of collections for families to view at home; on-line access to information about a museum's vertebrate paleontology collection may save or prompt a visit to the institution by a scholar.

People are probably most easily seduced by the power and capabilities of technology as a source of information. They begin to dream of huge databases containing images of all the museum's collections, shown at different angles, in 3-D, and maybe even in animated or video segments. But museums must remember to match the format and content with the needs and interests of users. We can't assume that "if we build it, they will come." Not only is this a naive and dangerous way to allocate resources, but we run the risk of using technology in ways that alienate or overwhelm visitors.

Where Philosophy Meets Practice: Two Stories

The OH!Canada Project • Art Gallery of Ontario

In 1995, the Art Gallery of Ontario in Toronto, Canada, launched a large project that combined art, technology, and the public (Worts 1997). Much more than an art exhibition, it was billed as "the Gallery's first-time-ever, interactive, multimedia, 'you're gonna love it' art event—starring the Group of Seven, leading Canadian artists and you." OH!Canada was a blockbuster of a very different sort. Essentially, it aimed to explore two themes—environment and identity— from historical and contemporary perspectives. It was believed that the project could use the visual arts to create a resonant link between the past and the present, using themes that have been relevant for a long time.

The historical anchor of the project featured an exhibition of stunning landscape paintings by the Group of Seven (Canada's best-known artists) to mark the 75th anniversary of their first exhibition. The group is renowned for its efforts to capture the very essence of Canadian identity in landscapes of the country. Group members also were sensitive to the many forces that threatened the natural environment.

A second component was a three-part exhibit/forum on the question of "What Makes a Nation: People? Stories? Lands?" in which artworks from 1930 to 1995 were used to explore how artists have reflected on the same themes as the Group of Seven, but with very different results—reflecting changing times. Critical to this installation was the use of video recordings of interviews with a wide cross-section of people who spoke about their experiences of Canada. Included were long-time residents, Native Canadians, recent immigrants, children, and seniors. They expressed their thoughts in English, French, Italian, and Mandarin. These testimonials provided questions, provocation, and insights on the subject of "What makes a nation?," as interview subjects discussed special places, memorable stories, and important people. Three video monitors—one each for "Stories?," "People?," and "Land?"—were embedded in tables with pencils and cards available for visitors to record their own responses. Other visitors could then browse though the cards.

The most radical, contemporary, and engaging part of the project was the OH!Canada Workshop, which filled the second-largest exhibition hall in the museum. About two-thirds of the space was given over to six community groups and six schools, each of which created an art installation reflecting on the themes of identity and the natural environment. The community groups were not representative of the gallery's traditional audience. Included were four First Nations artists, a traditional Chinese brush painting school, an adult English as a Second Language (ESL) class, a storefront community arts group from a Toronto neighborhood, and a group of Latino teenagers who cover the city with graffiti. The participating schools (including elementary, secondary, and college-level institutions) spent three months studying the themes in class and finding a way to express both individual and collective responses to them.

Beyond these installations, a large space was available for audience participation. At a 30-foot long table, visitors could write, draw, color, cut, and paste on "Make Your Mark" cards, which were then displayed on a big "Share Your Reaction" wall. On a wall of equal dimension was a gigantic blackboard on which visitors could write and draw their reactions. A local television station, BRAVO!, provided a "Speakers Corner," which recorded on video the comments of the public, which were then selectively aired on television, as well as edited and run on video monitors in the exhibit space. Using the somewhat older technology of fax machines, schools and the public alike were encouraged to send their writings and images. Many of the public reactions were elicited by a "Question of the Week" (such as "Is Canada falling apart, or just growing up?," "What symbols of Canada have meaning for you?," "What do you love and hate about Canada?"). These questions were developed by a team that reviewed all public responses and tried to respond to issues raised by the discourse.

All these facets of the project were also integrated into the gallery's new World Wide Web site. The site was designed to provide rich information on the project, as well an invitation to respond to its themes. The "Question of the Week" figured prominently on the site and was directly connected to an open-ended database in which users from anywhere in the world (but especially Canada) could feel comfortable browsing other submissions and contributing their own.

This very active approach to the OH!Canada Project represents the Art Gallery of Ontario's attempt to turn away from the more narrow public programming that has characterized art museums for such a long time. A balance was sought between the quiet, reflective spaces in a compelling exhibition and the dynamic exchange of a lively forum. The past became better connected to the present, and the present provided a motivational gateway into new explorations of the past. Many responses surfaced. Some patrons felt much more comfortable within the walls of the museum during this period, while other regular visitors felt that their sanctuary had been partially invaded. Controversy also arose when some members of the public overtly—and comfortably—expressed racism and intolerance in contributions to the forum. The museum realizes that it will take some effort to really understand how best to manage the dynamics of combining the concept of the temple and the forum. Yet, for all that is still to be achieved, the OH!Canada Project represents one of the more aggressive efforts to use technology when expanding the museum experience into areas where it rarely ventures.

Hockey Hall of Fame • Toronto, Canada

The new Hockey Hall of Fame in Toronto re-invented itself in 1993, becoming a powerful example of how objects, stories, technology-based exhibits, and visitors can be brought together in a balanced way creating an experience that is both personal and collective. Using trophies (the Stanley Cup is always on view and is touchable!), photos, and details about hockey stars, the shrine function of the hall encourages individuals to explore and pay homage to the people whose skills have inspired youth to develop their own potential. In this space, visitors' personal associations with professional hockey help create an intense and usually affirming moment.

The lion's share of space is dedicated to interactive, information-rich exhibits designed as a series of "zones." One particularly popular area is a full-scale reproduction of the Montreal Canadiens dressing room. Visitors can touch authentic clothing and equipment while they watch a 12-minute video of the Montreal players preparing to go onto the ice for a National Hockey League game. As the video ends with a call for the players to enter the arena, a set of double doors springs open and visitors exit into a room that feels like an arena. The sensation of "being there" is enhanced by a blast of cold air, rubberized flooring underfoot, and a recording of an enthusiastic crowd. A sophisticated sports medicine display using multimedia exhibit technology extends the experience of the "Dressing Room Zone." It is truly a multi-sensory, imaginative experience.

The "North American Zone" offers an in-depth look at the many amateur and professional hockey leagues that operate on this continent. Using interactive, multimedia technology along with a large map of Canada and the United States, visitors can access information about the many variations of hockey found in this part of the world. People from all over North America are invited to submit their team photographs and logos for inclusion in an ever-growing visual

Toronto's Hockey Hall of Fame has interactive, information-rich exhibits. Photo by Kristine Morrissey.

database, which showcases some of the intensely personal ways in which individuals make hockey part of their own lives.

At the new Hockey Hall of Fame, as at similar institutions, visitors learn about hockey through significant historical objects, touch-screen information kiosks, and engaging environments. But they also actively participate in the fundamentals of hockey itself with the help of sophisticated technology. Two extraordinary exhibits exemplify this aspect of the hall. In the first, the visitor, with pads and hockey stick in hand, stands in front of a goalie net, as professional hockey players shoot pucks at him or her. But the pucks that fly do not endanger the would-be goalie because this exhibit relies on virtual reality. Despite the absence of a real puck, visitors get to feel what it's like to be a goalie. In the second exhibit, visitors can test their skill by stepping onto simulated ice and shooting pucks at video-projected goalies. Computers calculate the speed and direction of each puck and let visitors know if they scored. The pucks and sticks in this exhibit are the real thing, and the physical experience offered here is a great complement to the more cerebral nature of other installations.

A highlight of any visit is a stop at the television network exhibit. Here, banks of monitors, miles of cable, and a robotics producer offer visitors a behind-the-scenes view of a televised hockey broadcast. Visitors who are brave enough can test their skill as television announcers. A high-tech broadcast booth gives people a chance to watch a great moment in professional hockey, while a professional announcer provides commentary. Then, the action is replayed without commentary; printed prompts tell which player has the puck at any given second. Visitors can then announce the play into a microphone, and their efforts are played back for them to hear. It is great fun and yet another example of a non-traditional interpretive strategy in an exhibition.

Final Thoughts

The best way to predict the future is to invent it.

—Alan Kay
quoted in The Art of Human-Computer Interface Design

What is the real challenge for museums in the information age? Is it learning how to use new technologies and keeping up with rapid developments? Is it changing our perspective from reflections on the past to projections of the future? The real challenge, which will shape our identity and our future, lies in considering not just the technology or the tools, but the individual, the group, our cultures, and our institutions. The real challenge is in better understanding how technology can illuminate and enhance the complex relationships between people and objects.

At its best, technology can facilitate experiences in which visitors can both transcend and live more fully in their daily lives, thoughts, and activities. It can challenge visitors to reconsider or create new meanings. It can help visitors see their experiences in a context that connects them to other people, places, and times. It can help museums realize their institutional potential as they help people realize their individual potential. The final challenge then is no less than that of placing technology in the service of understanding and enhancing the human experience.

References

American Association of Museums. 1992. *Excellence and equity: Education and the public dimension of museums*. Washington, D.C.: American Association of Museums.

Cameron, Duncan F. 1971. The museum: a temple or the forum. *Curator* 14, no. 1: 11-24.

Csikszentmihályi, Mihály and Hermanson, Kim. 1995. Intrinsic motivation in museums: What makes visitors want to learn? *Museum News* 74, no. 3: 34-37, 59-62.

Falk, John H. and Lynn D. Dierking. 1992. *The museum experience*. Washington, D.C.: Whalesback Books.

Glaser, Jane R. and Artemis A. Zenetou, eds. 1994. *Gender perspectives: Essays on women in museums*. Washington, D.C.: Smithsonian Institution Press.

McLean, Kathleen. 1993. *Planning for people in museum exhibitions*. Washington, D.C.: Association of Science–Technology Centers.

Naisbitt, John. 1982. *Megatrends*. New York: Warner Books, Inc.

Perry, Deborah. 1994. The anatomy of a museum visit: What visitors really want. In *The sourcebook: 1994 annual meeting*. Washington, D.C.: American Association of Museums.

Postman, Neil. 1992. *Technopoly*. New York, New York: Vintage Books.

Rheingold, Howard. 1991. *Virtual reality*. New York: A Touchstone Book, Simon & Schuster.

Silverman, Lois H. 1995. Visitor meaning-making in museums for a new age. *Curator* 38, no. 3: 161–170.

Talbott, Stephen L. 1995. *The future does not compute: Transcending the machines in our midst*. Sebastopol, Calif.: O'Reilly & Associates, Inc.

Tilden, Freeman. 1957. *Interpreting our heritage*. Chapel Hill, N.C.: The University of North Carolina Press.

Worts, Douglas. 1997. Assessing the risks and potentials of the OH!Canada Project. *MUSE* 15, no. 2: 19-30.

_____. 1995. Extending the frame: Forging a new partnership with the public. In *Art in museums*. Edited by Susan Pearce. London: Athlone Press: 165-191.

Wurman, Richard Saul. 1989. *Information anxiety*. New York: Bantam Books.

chapter 11

Going Electronic: A Case Study of "Ocean Planet" and Its On-line Counterpart

Judith Gradwohl and Gene Feldman

Introduction

When it opened in April 1995, "Ocean Planet Online" (http://seawifs.gsfc.nasa.gov/ocean_planet.html) became the Smithsonian Institution's first exhibition available through the World Wide Web. Developed as an electronic counterpart to "Ocean Planet," a major traveling exhibition, "Ocean Planet Online" is a translation of exhibition content to the Web. As such, it presents an excellent opportunity to examine issues of content and media in museums.

"Ocean Planet Online" is an adaptation of material designed for presentation in the linear format of a museum gallery. In producing the on-line version, we faced the problems of translating elements designed for the physical experience of visiting a museum, including presenting a coherent storyline in a directionless medium and adapting exhibits that were essentially visual or interactive for the "small screen." We needed to provide navigational aids for users who could enter from anywhere in the exhibition. The fact that we were designing material for an undefined or, at least, a little-known

Judith Gradwohl, an exhibition curator and scientist, directs the Smithsonian Without Walls program of the National Museum of American History, Washington, D.C. She served as curator of "Ocean Planet." Gene Feldman is an oceanographer at the NASA/Goddard Space Flight Center, Greenbelt, Md., who makes use of the World Wide Web and other emerging technologies for public education. He created the "Ocean Planet Online" Web site.

audience complicated the job. Finally, we were very interested in giving users an experience that approximated a visit to the physical exhibition.

We found that we were more successful with some of these efforts than others, that some were not even worth attempting, and that, in some instances, we were able to incorporate material that did not fit in the physical show. We also learned a great deal about our audience and Web site design. Our experiences have led us in directions we did not foresee when we began this project.

"Ocean Planet," the Traveling Exhibition

"Ocean Planet" was the culmination of a four-year effort by the Smithsonian Institution's Environmental Awareness Program to study and understand issues affecting the health of the world's oceans. It was on view at the National Museum of Natural History for one year beginning in April 1995, and then began a three-year national tour.

"Ocean Planet" was concept-driven rather than based upon objects from the National Museum of Natural History's collections. The exhibit team, led by Curator Judith Gradwohl, first defined the issues to be presented, then developed a storyline, and finally collected objects and images to illustrate the concepts. After conducting visitor studies in Washington, D.C., Chicago, and Denver, we determined that the museum-going audience already had some basic familiarity with environmental issues affecting the oceans. Thus, the exhibition was designed to reinforce or validate visitors' general knowledge and help them understand the wide range of issues that affect the health of the oceans. The exhibition had a definitive message: All of our lives rely upon healthy oceans, and our actions on land affect the health of the oceans.

The 6,000-square-foot exhibition comprised an introductory walkway and five major galleries. Traffic flow was unidirectional, and most of the visitors entered through the entrance and left through the exit.

In the first major gallery, "Ocean Science," exhibits featured information on the diversity of life in the oceans, the effect of ocean current on climate, oceanographic research, and conditions in the deep sea. We intended this gallery to spark excitement about the riches of the seas, provide an introduction to the science underlying decisions about marine environmental policy, and show some of the ways the oceans affect life on land. Exhibits employed video, audio, animation, sculpture, and models, as well as text and photo panels.

In "Sea People," we introduced people whose lives and livelihoods take them to sea, and showed that many people depend directly on the oceans. The focal point of the gallery was a video presentation. Incorporating music and poetry, the video featured a diverse array of seafarers and was complemented by exhibit cases containing objects from a number of seafaring societies. The cases showed that although seafarers are diverse there are many similarities between seafaring cultures—in the tightly knit nature of seafaring societies, in the knowledge people gain as they go to sea, and in the risks they constantly face.

The "Sea Store" gallery showed that even the lives of people who are not seafarers relate to the oceans. Exhibits illustrated ties to the oceans through seafood, products containing marine components, medicines, global economics, and recreation. They also showed how the oceans have intrinsic and aesthetic value. We conveyed these messages through a number of different media including a computer interactive program, specimens, models, photo, and text panels.

"Oceans in Peril" featured large photomurals of beautiful scenes representing various marine ecosystems and large "marker buoys" that displayed examples of four different types of threats to the oceans: pollution, habitat alteration, over-fishing, and global issues of population and development. Each of the 20 faces on the buoys presented a specific environmental issue, showed a case study of its effects, and illustrated ways that the particular threat was being addressed. At the end of the gallery we presented profiles of people who are working to solve marine conservation problems, showing that they look much like the average museum visitor. The message was that not all conservationists are fanatics and that help is valuable at a number of levels.

The final gallery, entitled "Reflections," featured a large, striking sculpture of Earth with the land masses and oceans encrusted with costume jewelry and beads. It emphasized the vast extent and value of the oceans. We also provided information about how museum visitors could become involved with ocean conservation. And literature and CD-ROM stations gave more detailed information about exhibition-related topics.

Translating the Exhibition to the Web

The idea for an on-line version of "Ocean Planet" originated with Gene Feldman, an oceanographer and project advisor from the National Aeronautics and Space Administration (NASA). In spring 1994, when he first suggested that we attempt to put the exhibition on-line, project staff had never seen nor heard of the World Wide Web. After plans for the exhibition passed the 50-percent review, we began discussions about what it would require to put the exhibition on-line. It was not until after the 95-percent review in August 1994, when Feldman offered to take on all of the programming and production personally, that we began the project.

The entire cost for "Ocean Planet Online" was $1,200. These funds went toward a contract for a graphic designer, who helped refine the look of the program one month before it was launched. All of the programming was done on a volunteer basis by Feldman and Norman Kuring at NASA, and many photographers and artists generously allowed their commercial work, on display in "Ocean Planet," to be used in the on-line version without additional charge. This tremendous level of cooperation and volunteerism made it possible to create a complex program over a relatively short period of time and essentially without a budget.

Because we waited to begin developing "Ocean Planet Online" until late in the overall process, the physical exhibition was well under development. At the Smithsonian Institution, the 95-percent review comes after the script is complete, almost all of the visuals and objects are in-hand, and the design and installation blueprints are 95-percent complete. The script could only be changed to correct mistakes, and the entire exhibition and our vision of the visitor experience were well mapped out.

"Ocean Planet Online" was shaped significantly by the decisions made during the planning for "Ocean Planet." The content, design, and script were based on what we knew about audiences in natural history museums, with an emphasis on the Smithsonian audience. The exhibition had a strong narrative and a linear storyline designed to develop specific themes. The designers had selected colors, typefaces, and materials that reflected the themes in each gallery and shaped our expectations of the look and feel of the exhibition. We wrote the text with a hierarchy of importance in mind: large, concise headlines that provided the main messages, text of 50 words or less that elaborated on the headlines, and focus labels and captions that interpreted objects and graphics. The voice was authoritative but accessible. The format of the graphics conformed with the size and shape of panels, and we designed the illustrations to be silk-screened using a maximum of two or three colors.

We had specific goals for "Ocean Planet Online." The rationale was to make the content of "Ocean Planet" available to people, nationally and internationally, who were unlikely to be able to visit the exhibition at a host museum. We also felt that the online presentation would allow us to use some of the research and material that were not available in the exhibition because of space, time, and budget constraints. In designing the on-line experience, we wanted to give users the sense that they were visiting the exhibition at the National Museum of Natural History. Finally, we felt that "Ocean Planet Online" could serve as a resource by providing a conduit to ocean-related information available elsewhere on the World Wide Web, and that it had the potential to excite users about a variety of marine topics and provide multiple options for further study.

Although we jumped into developing "Ocean Planet Online" without much forethought about how well a three-dimensional, experiential exhibition would translate into this new medium, we soon realized that the effort was going to require more than a quick redesign. We began by digitizing all of the "Ocean Planet" resources: the final script, the images, and any exhibition-related graphic materials. This was a tremendous undertaking by the two NASA programmers, and it was done without the aid of Web-authoring software. After we felt we had satisfactorily provided the content and some of the feel of the exhibition, we focused on functionality, user orientation, and ancillary information that could provide greater content depth. Finally, just before the launch, we hired a designer to help refine the look and redesign some of the exhibition graphics for the on-line medium.

The conflict between aesthetics and load time loomed as a major issue from the start. We tried presenting panels more or less in their entirety and using large (half-screen) formats for the images, many of which were spectacular and presented in very large formats within the physical exhibition. Although the brief text allowed an entire panel to be presented on a single, not-too-intimidating, page, most often we presented only thumbnail-sized photographs and tried to intimate the hierarchy of information by changing type size and leaving spaces between text blocks.

The organization of "Ocean Planet Online" is as linear as the physical exhibition, but this is only evident in the lengthy topic outline that lists all of the main pages in the program. Most Web users prefer to meander through material, so we needed to provide a means of orientation that would allow users to understand where they were within the mass of information available on the site. We wanted users to be able to wander freely down any series of links and yet be able to find their way back to familiar territory.

Ironically, the physical layout of "Ocean Planet" provided a valuable navigation tool for "Ocean Planet Online." We decided to use the floor plan of the physical exhibition as an orientation device because we could not come up with any more logical system and we were already very comfortable with the show's floor plan. The floor plan is more than a simple map of the content. It shows each of the major galleries in "Ocean Planet" and their relationships to each other, and it suggests the relative importance of the topics by high-lighting the different sizes of the galleries. The only modification to the floor plan for "Ocean Planet Online" was the addition of "swim-ming" fish, which show users the entrance, the order of the galleries, and the exit. We repeated the fish symbol at the bottom of each page; if a user finds herself down an unwanted path, a click on the fish will make the floor plan reappear. Studies of "Ocean Planet Online" users have shown that many return several times to the floor plan during a visit, which indicates that people are using it in the manner we intended.

Elements in "Ocean Planet Online" and Their Origin

Some material translated easily from "Ocean Planet" to "Ocean Planet Online," other components required significant alterations, and still others were unique to the on-line presentation. As might be expected, some elements worked better in the physical exhibition while others were more suitable for the on-line program.

Direct Translations: The text, images, and accompanying printed materials from "Ocean Planet" were the easiest to adapt for "Ocean Planet Online." The on-line program contains all of the text from "Ocean Planet," most of which we assembled into pages representing panels and other individual physical exhibit elements. It incorporates 80 percent of the 232 photographs used in the exhibition and, because we did not have a budget for developing "Ocean Planet Online," all of the images are presented courtesy of the rights-owners.

We worked with a variety of photographers to determine an acceptable format for use of the commercial images. NASA programmers developed a "watermark" that they electronically embedded in the image to discourage downloading for print purposes, and we degraded the quality of the photos so that they were all presented with a maximum dimension of 384 pixels. Most of the photographs are presented as thumbnails (75 pixels as maximum dimension), which users can enlarge to the maximum dimension.

We relied heavily on Smithsonian-owned photographs of the "Ocean Planet" installation in the National Museum of Natural History, both to provide the look and feel of the physical exhibition and as an introduction to many galleries. The installation photographs transport users from an aerial floor plan to the point of view of visitors standing in the exhibition.

Ten video presentations are included in "Ocean Planet Online," as short, 10-second segments. We only presented video footage from the public domain (much of which was not in "Ocean Planet") because of the issues we encountered with the still photos. Short audio segments of music and sounds are also available.

Most of the printed matter that accompanied "Ocean Planet" is also available on "Ocean Planet Online." This includes fact sheets, educational materials, and excerpts from accompanying publications. We also linked lesson plans developed for "Ocean Planet" and other curricula that cover related topics to pages within the online version so that teachers could take electronic field trips and download work sheets and background information. The availability of teaching material on-line has an added benefit of saving staff time and museum funds that might be spent filling requests for photocopies, because now teachers can download and print anything that interests them.

Alterations: Many elements, including exhibit cases and experiential or interactive components, required significant alteration for presentation in "Ocean Planet Online." One of the most popular elements in the physical exhibition was the "product pyramid" in the "Sea Store." Visitors could use an ersatz light pen and "read" bar codes from products available in any supermarket: food, beverages, toiletries, cleaning products, and others. The four-sided display case held 48 different products. A computer monitor displayed the components in the products that came from the oceans. In "Ocean Planet Online," we wanted to preserve the element of surprise and the interactive nature of the exhibit. NASA programmers conceived the idea of using a random-number generator that would present one of the 48 products each time a user clicked on the bar code.

Translating objects in exhibit cases to the Web also presented a challenge. The appeal of artifacts in the physical museum setting is partly due to their three-dimensionality and partly to their being "the real thing." Objects are selected based on their capacity to express exhibition themes and also because they present aesthetic or intriguing groupings. While we were developing "Ocean Planet Online," the technology did not exist to group objects and text on a page without turning the entire page into an excruciatingly slow-loading graphic. We decided to present the objects in groups by creating a collage of their images. We did not display the focus labels with the objects unless a user clicked on a particular object and, at that point, only one object label would be available at a time. Throughout the program, whenever we presented somewhat cryptic information such as graphics without accompanying text, we included on the bottom of the same page either a list of options that the graphics could lead to or an outline of the material that the graphics represented.

Most visits to museums are social experiences, while most computer users operate in solitude. To preserve an element of social interactivity and provide a forum for enthusiasts to discuss the oceans, we developed a bulletin board as part of the resource room. This also served as a comment and suggestion book as well as a place for "visitors" to interact. From the exhibit team's perspective, this user-to-user communication also may have stemmed the flow of many e-mail queries to exhibit staff that we were too short-staffed to answer.

The Web site also has links to the Smithsonian Institution museum shops' catalogue offerings. Making purchases directly from "Ocean Planet Online" is not possible, but the shop pages provide a toll-free phone number and catalogue purchasing information. This feature was added because there was a museum shop in the exhibition floor plans and catalogue information that was ready to go on-line. We did not intend it to be a revenue-generating element. However, the on-line shop does get requests from many visitors, similar to the way most people will take a quick look in the museum shops when they visit a physical museum.

Additions: The on-line medium can accommodate several levels of information tailored to specific interests, and we took advantage of this feature in developing our on-line presentation. Much of the material that is unique to "Ocean Planet Online" strengthens its value as a resource about ocean science and conservation. In a few cases we included material that was cut from the physical exhibition due to lack of space. Finally, the inclusion of numerous links to other Web sites directed users to other sources of ocean-related information.

Programmers at NASA wrote a code for searches that would allow users to search all of "Ocean Planet Online" for images and text that related to a specific topic. Although searches became more commonly available after "Ocean Planet Online" opened, the searches developed for the program were considered among the site's unique features when the program premiered in spring 1995.

One search engine uses a photo archive and allows users to browse through all of the graphics available in the program. Users also can search by using key words found in related caption material.

We also were interested in showing some of the scholarship that went into developing "Ocean Planet." The script on file in the exhibit team offices has 400 footnotes that show the sources of facts used in the exhibition. Although this information was not available in the exhibition gallery, it is available through links from "Ocean Planet Online." We included this feature "because it was there," and it appears that some users spend a significant amount of time looking up the footnotes.

The curator's tours reflect an attempt to satisfy users who might be uncomfortable with the on-line medium. Many users had not yet learned to click fearlessly, and we wanted to provide a piece of the program that would appeal to the rank technology novice. The tours developed by the NASA programmers provide a directed look at the mass of material in "Ocean Planet." Users can choose from a few prearranged tours and "visit" the exhibition, viewing a series of screens where they only need to click "next" to keep moving. Although this heavily directed use of a Web site is somewhat antithetical to the free-wheeling ethic of the World Wide Web, the feature has received a moderate amount of use.

A calendar of events provided a direct link between the physical and electronic exhibitions during its tenure at the National Museum of Natural History. It listed all of the public events, including those related to "Ocean Planet."

Another hallmark of "Ocean Planet Online" is the extensive amount of statistical information that is available. Detailed data about the use of "Ocean Planet Online" is available in text and graphic formats that summarize when the site is used, from which country or domain users originate, which pages, graphics, and other features users requested most frequently, and even Internet provider (IP) addresses of the top 50 requesters each month.

"Ocean Planet Online" User Study

As of January 1997, after 1.7 years on-line, "Ocean Planet Online" had been visited by more than 400,000 unique computers, which may represent 800,000 to 1,200,000 users. The program had shipped out over 170 gigabytes of material. The Smithsonian's Institutional Studies Office worked with NASA programmers to capture and analyze data about use of "Ocean Planet Online."[1] They analyzed 2,020 "visits" (separate logins by unique IP addresses separated by more than two hours). The sample size represents 7 percent of the total visits made to "Ocean Planet Online" between Aug. 31, 1995, and Nov. 1, 1995.

Most of the visits (1,813 out of 2,020) were new logins. The remainder were repeat visits by the same machines; on average, a machine would "visit" the site 10 times. Remember that IP addresses represent individual computers or "gateways" that bundle requests from members of subscription services. As such, we cannot determine from an analysis of IP addresses whether the same individuals re-visited "Ocean Planet Online."

On average a visit consisted of 4.9 stops (or page requests) per address, but nearly 40 percent of the visits consisted of only a single stop, while 14 percent made two stops. The maximum number of stops for an individual visit was 66. Two-thirds of the visits came via the home page, and one-third landed somewhere in the middle of the program from an outside link or previously set bookmark. "Drop-in" visitors were more likely to make only a single stop in "Ocean Planet Online" than the visitors who entered through the "front door."

Calculating a mean visit time required correcting for situations where visitors may have walked away from the computer or accessed another Web site frame without exiting "Ocean Planet Online." The mean visit time was 6.8 minutes ($\pm$ 10 minutes) and the median visit time was 1.9 minutes. Average stop time was 94 seconds ($\pm$ 134 seconds).

Visitors used every section of the exhibition and all of the features. The pages that received the most use were the home page (1,575 visits) and the floor plan (1,830). During prolonged use of "Ocean Planet Online," visitors used the floor plan repeatedly as a navigation device. Users made more visits (1,164) to the "Ocean Science" section than to other content of the exhibition; for example 431 visits were made to "Oceans in Peril" and 200 were made to the

"Sea Store." A surprisingly large number of visitors (935) made use of the tours. By comparison, the most popular exhibit in "Ocean Planet," the product pyramid in the "Sea Store," was visited by 92.3 percent of 246 visitors followed in a tracking study.

That is intriguing at a number of levels. It is unusual to find any data quantifying use of Web sites beyond the highly unsatisfying measurement of "hits." Most Web-tracking software follows hits because they are a very straightforward measurement of the amount of information requested by a user. However they are not a good indication of relative use of different sites because the number of hits depends upon the design of Web pages and the amount of information users are forced to load when they request a page. Hits measure every type of information that was transferred, including icons, lines, and other graphic elements that are not specifically requested by users.

The "Ocean Planet Online" study indicates a tremendous potential for applying some of the techniques we use to study visitors in physical museums to learn more about Web-based audiences. Study results imply that we may have several distinct audiences visiting Web sites, including: new visitors, repeat visitors, and "front-door" and "drop-in" visitors. The results also imply that we may have a limited number of screens in which to convey information to most users. Finally, they indicate that visitors on-line make different use of exhibition material than visitors to our physical galleries.

What We Learned about Site Design

Very early in the project we realized that the conversion of "Ocean Planet" to "Ocean Planet Online" was far more complicated than moving from three dimensions to two. When we first began working on the on-line project, most Web sites were linear in essence, allowing users to move between points on an outline through the magic of hyper-links. However, we felt that the sites that were set up like books were about as interesting but far more difficult to read. Although we were unwilling to abandon the linear story structure of the exhibition and the look and feel of the physical show, we tried to make it possible to bypass our narrative and still have a meaningful experience.

Moving on-line required us to change our expectations of the audience. In museum exhibits, and especially at the Smithsonian, we usually have only one chance at a visitor walking through an exhibition. Our goals in shaping a physical exhibition are to persuade the visitors to slow down and take in as much of the material as possible on a single visit. Although the average amount of time a person spent in the 6,000-square-foot "Ocean Planet" exhibition was 11 minutes, the material could easily sustain a visit of 45 minutes or longer. Thus we conceived, wrote, and designed the original show to encourage visitors to stay as long as possible.[2]

Furthermore, most museum visitors walk all the way through an exhibition even if they are just trying to find the exit. Exhibit headlines, varying display techniques, and changing colors and moods in various galleries all convey messages as the visitor walks by, even if he does not linger long enough to read the text. Visitors to most museums have gone to some trouble to get there (or they've found that impossible parking place), so they are likely to spend some time justifying the commitment of their time and resources.

All that changes on-line. Visitors can drop in and out of an on-line exhibition and any other Web site with ease. It is as though museum visitors could shoot through the roof with any given step in an exhibition. To compound this expectation of a truncated time commitment, the culture of Web surfing does not encourage the type of in-depth attention to a topic that reading or other media can promote.

These issues merely hint at the potential for new and unexpected audience behavior and expectations museum professionals encounter when they design Web sites. In museums we actively study our audience demographics and desires and even include audience surveys as a necessary first step when developing an idea for an exhibition. As we switch to this new and little-studied medium, we know very little about who our audiences are and even less about what they are looking for in a Web site.

When we began to work on "Ocean Planet Online," researchers were just starting to compile the demographics of Web users. In late 1994 we faced an audience comprised mostly of men between the ages of 20 and 40, who had Internet access through universities and research groups. After a few months, a fairly long time span in terms of the World Wide Web, the audience changed significantly. More women began using the Web, the age range expanded considerably, more homes and schools began to be wired, and transmission speeds improved substantially. The rapid change in audience demographics and in their expectations of Web sites continues today. This continual change means that the World Wide Web audience is a moving target. If we tailor an on-line program for a specific audience, it might be completely off-target in a matter of months.

We understood that we would not have the same firm grasp on the audience for "Ocean Planet Online" as we have in physical museums, so we tried to appeal to a wide range of users. We made many assumptions about the audience in developing the on-line exhibit. By using the same text and images as we used in the exhibit hall, we were aiming at a typical natural history museum audience, i.e., relatively well-educated and middle-class families.

The move to cyberspace also calls for consideration of the notion of community. Except for the small number of adults who visit exhibits alone (at the Smithsonian this averages around 15 percent of the visitor population), all museum visits have a social component. In fact, visitor studies have shown that social interactions can enhance the quality of a visit and encourage educational experiences. A truly successful label is one that visitors feel compelled to share with someone by reading it to them aloud.[3] By contrast, computer use is a relatively solitary activity. And it is frustrating to visit a Web site when somebody else has control of the mouse. However, with the proliferation of chat rooms, multi-user dimensions (MUDs), and bulletin board systems (BBS), there can be a strong sense of community on-line and many opportunities for interactions with other users. Because of the international and dispersed nature of the Web, the on-line community is broader than the museum community, but communication consists of momentary exchanges between strangers.

The quality of offerings on the World Wide Web has improved considerably since we began this project, but it still varies considerably. With the large quantity of transparent links in "Ocean Planet Online," we were concerned that users know when they were visiting the Smithsonian Institution and when they were looking at pages produced elsewhere. We carefully vetted the links but had no control over those within the sites to which our site was connected, and we knew that we could never monitor all of the material on each linked site. We tried to develop a distinctive look and designed a banner for the top of each page that would help show the difference between information provided by the Smithsonian and that provided by others. It turned out that the banner added too much load time to many of pages, and we abandoned it as a standard format. In recent years new browsers have made it possible to add images that give a site a distinctive look yet do not take a great deal of time to load.

Nonetheless, as museums create more offerings on the World Wide Web, we need to consider the issue of authority. Traditionally museums have been bastions of the truth, and most visitors feel that they are receiving carefully conceived and factually correct information in museum exhibits. On the Web, however, anyone can initiate a museum and, in many cases, even draw material from other museum sites. Established institutions may need to consider how to distinguish their offerings from those not tied to collections, curators, educators, and the wide range of expertise housed in physical museums. Both the Web and Web-based culture are egalitarian in nature, and users are more accustomed to participating in content decisions. Presentations on the Web are likely to be more well-received if they avoid authoritarian tones, incorporate user views, and present open-ended material.

For a museum curator used to producing large, time-consuming, and expensive exhibitions, a foray onto the Web can be liberating. Although at the Smithsonian we conduct visitor studies to evaluate the effectiveness of exhibitions, we rarely have funds to make major revisions after the exhibition opens. In practice, unless a major factual, political, or fiscal mistake is made, all of the exhibit elements, graphics, and text that are complete at the 95-percent review are installed in the gallery until the exhibition closes. Revisions are very carefully considered and usually accomplished with least expense. It is rare, however, for a member of the exhibit team to walk through the exhibition just before the opening and not notice a few things that he or she would do differently the next time.

Change is not only expected on the World Wide Web, users value it. A good site is never truly finished, and this is even reflected in the terminology used: We launch or open a site but never complete it. With "Ocean Planet Online," we had the luxury of taking a final, critical look at the program the day before it opened, and we made some significant changes. With any project developed over an extended period, revisiting decisions that are months old is difficult or even impossible. For Web-based programs, self-criticism and a willingness to make revisions are highly advisable.

With the availability of Web-authoring software and high-quality images, it could appear that museums are well suited to generate on-line counterparts to all of their exhibitions. Although the initial uneasiness about Web sites competing with the real things in our collections and galleries has abated, museums still should consider their goals in producing on-line programs. Web sites can encourage and enhance a visit to a physical museum by introducing material and providing logistical information. Web sites can expand the museum's audience by providing a channel of communication with people who traditionally are not museum visitors. Ideally, museum sites can give the public high-quality educational offerings.

With the proliferation of high-quality Web sites, Web-based offerings from museums are no longer inexpensive and easy. We need to approach them with the same level of professionalism as we do productions in the exhibit halls. Very few museums have in-house expertise for the design and production of sophisticated Web sites and would have difficulty meeting the high standards of commercial sites.

Conclusions

Despite our original intentions to recreate the experience of a visit to "Ocean Planet" on the World Wide Web, we learned that resisting the urge to create an on-line replicate of a physical exhibition is best. This is even more true today than when we launched "Ocean Planet Online" in the relative infancy of recreational use of the World Wide Web. Although the content may translate easily, the structure of the narrative, the design, and even the voice may be inappropriate for the new medium.

The study of the use of "Ocean Planet Online" indicates that Web-site users may have shorter attention spans than museum visitors. This may require a change in the way we organize information for on-line presentations, and it has important design implications. On-line, it may be more vital to be efficient in presenting the main messages. Physical exhibitions often present background material to provide a foundation for understanding the themes. On-line it may be better to position the main themes before the background material. Additionally, a design that requires travel through four or five links to receive information may be less efficient than a design that requires fewer links.

The move from physical exhibitions to on-line presentations may require an entirely new metaphor. Many museum exhibitions are like three-dimensional books. The team develops a storyline that has an introduction, a plot or a message, and conclusions. Although visitors can and do wander randomly within an exhibition, they are generally encouraged to move unidirectionally, and galleries filled with related material are presented sequentially, like chapters in a book. Even in the most free-flowing exhibition, a great deal of thought goes into the clustering and ordering of objects and information.

Developing material for the Web is more like producing a landscape of information and helping users find trails of interest. It is somewhat analogous to the design of nature reserves in that there is a finite, delimited set of information or resources. Providing information and direction for visitors with a number of different interests is more important than arranging the resources so that everyone encounters similar assets. In fact, since Web site developers have even less ability to direct users than museum designers, it is unrealistic to try to provide much more than a clear understanding of the range of resources and an intuitive navigation system.

Although Web-based efforts ultimately could require as much effort and as many resources as physical exhibits, the World Wide Web presents a fascinating and important opportunity for museums. The key will be to take the best qualities of a museum visit and try to translate them so that they are effective in the new medium. While the offerings on the Web have grown more diverse and technologically exciting, high-quality content has lagged behind the technical and graphic capabilities. Museums and other educational institutions may find themselves well suited to further their educational missions by filling this void. We should see efforts like "Ocean Planet Online" as building blocks, but just as Web sites are never truly finished, all Web sites are essentially experimental efforts to respond to a rapidly evolving medium.

Acknowledgments

We would like to thank Norman Kuring, Beth Nalker, and Katherine Lenard for their assistance in developing the concepts and design of "Ocean Planet Online." Marc Pachter provided sorely needed moral and financial support. Zahava Doering and her staff at the Smithsonian Institution's Institutional Studies Office, particularly Andrew Pekarik, Steven Smith, and Adam Bickford, embraced the notion of studying "Ocean Planet Online." Kitty Connolly was a thoughtful reviewer and editor. This material is based on work supported by the National Science Foundation under Grant No. ESI-9254703. Additional funding was provided by The Pew Charitable Trusts, The Rockefeller Foundation, Geraldine R. Dodge Foundation, Smithsonian Institution, The David and Lucile Packard Foundation, National Ocean Industries Association, National Oceanic and Atmospheric Administration (NOAA) National Marine Fisheries Service, and Surdna Foundation, Inc. Chuck Molyneaux and Silicon Graphics, Inc., generously provided equipment and technical advice.

References

1. Smith, Steven J. January 1997. Smithsonian Institution Institutional Studies Office Working Paper. Washington, D.C.: Smithsonian Institution Institutional Studies Office.

2. Bickford, A., A. Pekarik, Z. Doering, and S. Yalowitz. 1996. Ocean views: A study of vistors to the "Ocean Planet" exhibition at the National Museum of Natural History. Washington, D.C.: Smithsonian Institution Institutional Studies Office.

3. Serrell, B. 1996. *Exhibit labels: An interpretive approach.* Walnut Creek, Calif.: Alta Mira Press.

chapter 12

Index

R

Relevance, 165
Repeated visits, 115
Reproductions, 81-82, 92, 98, 100-101
    see also   Facsimiles
Resources, 161

S

"Science in American Life," 163
Science Learning Network, 161
Science museums, 23–24, 158–159
"Seeds of Change," 61
"Shared Spaces, Separate Lives," 7–8
Signage, 140
Smithsonian Institution.
    See   National Museum of Natural
    History; National Zoo
"Smithsonian's America," 10–11
Social environment, 106–107
    see also   Environment; Public
    space
Sound, 141
Space, 131–133, 137–138
"Spirit of the Motherland," 62, 65, 66
Sports museums, 168–170
"A Step into the Past," 11–12
Storytelling, 25, 162
Surveys, 62, 182–184, 188–189
    pre-production, 134–135
    See also   Evaluation

T

Takeaway experience, 127
Technology, 74, 107–108, 155–157
    strategies for use, 157–165
Television, 82
Temple, museum as, 149–151
Text, 21
Thinking, 50–51
Think Tank, 50
Time, 63–64, 123
Tools and tool use, 51
Translation of exhibits.
    See   Development
Triangulation, 21

U

Updating, 142
User interface, 29
    see also   Interactivity; Media use
U.S. Holocaust Memorial Museum,
    22–23

V

Videos, 8
Videodiscs, 23, 24, 25–26, 76–77
Virtual museums, 83–85, 113–115
Visitor involvement, 13, 157–159
    see also   Audience; Interactivity;
    Media use
Visitor profile, 22–23
    see also   Evaluation; Surveys
Visually impaired, 22

W

Web sites, 108, 112, 114, 115, 116,
    173–190
"What about AIDS?" 62

Z

Zoos, 37–55